MW00647875

# doctrines

## A SIMPLIFIED ROAD MAP OF BIBLICAL TRUTH

by
**RAUL RIES**

**SLYP**
**somebody**
**loves you**
**publishing**
Diamond Bar, California

**Doctrines: A Simplified Road Map of Biblical Truth**
By Raul Ries
Copyright © 2009 by Somebody Loves You Media Group
Revised Edition © 2009

Published by Somebody Loves You Publishing
22324 Golden Springs Drive
Diamond Bar, CA 91765-2449


Library of Congress Control Number: 2009940199

---

---

For further information and resources contact:

Somebody Loves You Media Group
22324 Golden Springs Drive
Diamond Bar, CA 91765-2449
(800) 634-9165

slymediagroup@somebodylovesyou.com
www.somebodylovesyou.com

ISBN: 978-1-934820-15-5
Printed in the United States of America

Faith is not believing a thing without evidence; on the contrary faith rests upon the best evidence, namely the Word of God.

—Rev. William Evan

*The Great Doctrines of the Bible*

# TABLE OF CONTENTS

## Foreword

What we believe is of utmost importance, our spiritual life depends on it. In Paul's letters to Timothy, he mentions *doctrine* eleven times and *sound doctrine* twice. The importance of sound doctrine cannot be overemphasized. Raul has done a great service to the body of Christ, as he has set forth the basic doctrines of the faith, and gives us the Biblical reasons for why we believe what we believe. It is a must read, especially for new believers.

Pastor Chuck Smith
Calvary Chapel Costa Mesa

# A Word From Pastor Raul

As I look at the state of the world, I cannot help but think that we are living in the last days. Jesus said, in Matthew 24:4-8, when the Apostles asked for a sign:

> *"Take heed that no one deceives you. For many will come in My name, saying, 'I am the Christ,' and will deceive many. And you will hear of wars and rumors of wars. See that you are not troubled; for all these things must come to pass, but the end is not yet. For nation will rise against nation, and kingdom against kingdom. And there will be famines, pestilences, and earthquakes in various places. All these are the beginning of sorrows."*

As I look at the state of the church, I am concerned. As a shepherd, I worry that the sheep are not prepared and will be deceived. I talk to people in the church, and they do not even know the basic doctrines of the church; so I ask myself, "Have I not been diligent in teaching the flock the full counsel of the Lord?"

Through much prayer and seeking the Lord, He has led me to write this simple book on the great doctrines of the Bible. I feel my time is short, and I want to do all I can to serve the Lord and lead the flock which the Lord has entrusted to me.

Keep in mind—this is not an exhaustive study of the doctrines. There is so much more you can study on these great doctrines. I want to provide you with a simple guide, and you can take it from there. At the back of this book, you will find some suggested books for your own personal library—books that will help you know the Bible better and, in turn, know God better.

With your Bible and these tools, you will not be deceived. You will have an intimate relationship with Jesus Christ, and you will know the heartbeat of God.

May the Lord keep you, may He bless you and may His face shine upon you.

Souls for Christ,

Raul Ries

## INTRODUCTION
# Doctrine Is For Everyone

The word doctrine intimidates some people, for they think it is only for theologians. Others are turned off by the word doctrine, thinking it is divisive or irrelevant. But nothing could be further from the truth. According to the Bible, doctrine is something good, great and wonderful, and it is not just for an intellectual few—doctrine is for everyone!

The biblical words translated *doctrine* simply mean "teaching" or "instruction." Who of us should not want teaching or instruction in God's truth? Proverbs 8:33 says, *Hear instruction and be wise, and do not disdain it.* Proverbs 23:12 says, *Apply your heart to instruction, and your ears to words of knowledge.* Proverbs 9:9 says, *Give instruction to a wise man, and he will be still wiser; teach a just man, and he will increase in learning.* So learning doctrine should be something every believer desires and longs for.

The Scripture describes doctrine in a very positive way. The Bible refers to doctrine as being sound (2 Timothy 4:3; Titus 1:9, 2:1). The word for *sound* in the original language means "healthy, clean or whole." Doctrine is also referred to as good (1 Timothy 4:6). The word for *good* in the original means "wonderful, pleasing, attractive and beautiful." This is how we are to understand doctrine—as healthy, good, pleasing and wonderful.

As you study the uses of the word *doctrine* in the Bible, you discover its importance and benefits. The first and primary use of the Scriptures is to give us doctrine:

> *All Scripture is given by inspiration of God, and is profitable for doctrine, for reproof, for correction, for instruction in righteousness, that the man of God may be complete, thoroughly equipped for every good work* (2 Timothy 3:16-17).

The top priority of the early church was doctrine: *And they continued steadfastly in the apostles' doctrine and fellowship, in the breaking of bread, and in prayers* (Acts 2:42).

The whole of the Christian life is described as following doctrine: *But God be thanked that though you were slaves of sin, yet you obeyed from the heart that form of doctrine to which you were delivered* (Romans 6:17).

If we do not know doctrine, we can be easily misled:

> . . . *we should no longer be children, tossed to and fro and carried about with every wind of doctrine, by the trickery of men, in the cunning craftiness of deceitful plotting* (Ephesians 4:14).

In fact we are to stay away from those who do not teach sound doctrine: *Now I urge you, brethren, note those who cause divisions and offenses, contrary to the doctrine which you learned, and avoid them* (Romans 16:17).

This is why it is so essential for pastors to teach doctrine:

> *If you instruct the brethren in these things; you will be a good minister of Jesus Christ, nourished in the words of faith and of the good doctrine which you have carefully followed* (1 Timothy 4:6).

Understanding and knowing doctrine is more important now than ever before:

> *For the time will come when they will not endure sound doctrine, but according to their own desires, because they have itching ears, they will heap up for themselves teachers; and they will turn their ears away from the truth, and be turned aside to fables* (2 Timothy 4:3-4).

As Bible teacher Warren Wiersbe has well said:

> Today a modern, shallow attitude croons, "Don't give us doctrine, we just want practical truth from the heart." But such an approach would never have gotten to first base in the early church, let alone all the great preachers and teachers of church history. We need precision in doctrine just as much as we need precision in medicine, law, and mechanics. Can you imagine a sick man saying to his doctor, "Doc, it makes no difference whether you remove my appendix or my liver, just as long as I know that you care about me!" If devotional truth is not based on doctrinal truth, it is merely religious sentimentalism; and it will take more than a sentimental church to win the world to Jesus Christ!

With this in mind, let's consider the major doctrines of the Bible.

# Chapter 1

## DOCTRINE OF THE BIBLE
### BIBLIOLOGY

## A. The Need for the Scriptures

## B. The Inspiration of the Scriptures

1. Revelation
2. Inspiration
3. Illumination

## C. The Verification of the Scriptures

1. Internal
2. External

## D. The Canonicity and Authority of the Scriptures

1. Old Testament
2. The Apocrypha
3. New Testament

# Doctrine of the Bible
# BIBLIOLOGY
Greek words: *biblio* means "a book," and *ology,* "knowledge"

*The grass withers, the flower fades, Because the breath of the LORD blows upon it; Surely the people are grass. The grass withers, the flower fades, But the word of our God stands forever* (Isaiah 40:7-8).

## A. The Need for the Scriptures

In every Bible I own, I always write this quote as a constant reminder: "This Book will keep you from sin, but sin will keep you from this Book."

Why is it important to read the Bible? Through the inspired words of the Bible, God has revealed not only Himself, His plan for creation and salvation, but also His plan for you, personally, and your walk with Him. It is through God's Holy Word that we grow closer to God and learn of His character; only then can we live our lives consecrated to Him.

*All Scripture is given by inspiration of God, and is profitable for doctrine, for reproof, for correction, for instruction in righteousness, that the man of God may be complete, thoroughly equipped for every good work* (2 Timothy 3:16-17).

If we want to live our lives according to God's will, then we must be in His Word, so He can speak to us. Theologian John Murray put into perspective why we should live our lives according to God's Word when he said:

There is no situation in which we are placed, no demand that arises, for which Scripture as the deposit of the manifold wisdom of God is not adequate and sufficient.

Remember, there is no trial, no temptation, no tribulation you will face in your life that cannot be faced with God. It is through His Word that He will reveal Himself and His will for your life.

## B. The Inspiration of the Scriptures

*And so we have the prophetic word confirmed, which you do well to heed as a light that shines in a dark place, until the day dawns and the morning star rises in your hearts; knowing this first, that no prophecy of Scripture is of any private interpretation, for prophecy never came by the will of man, but holy men of God spoke as they were moved by the Holy Spirit* (2 Peter 1:19-21).

Webster defines *inspiration* as, "The supernatural influence of the Spirit of God on the human mind, by which prophets and apostles and sacred writers were qualified to set forth Divine truth without mixture of error."

By its very definition, we can conclude that all the writers of the books in the Bible were inspired by the Holy Spirit of God to write God's Word; and God provided verses within the Bible declaring its inspiration, because He knows the heart of man and the doubt that would arise.

These men lived during different periods of history and in different places, writing as they were led by the Spirit of God. They were holy men who wrote God's commands and eternal plans for man. So, the final product is God's truth that came from God Himself.

Many will tell you there are errors or inconsistencies in the Bible, but we know this cannot be true, because the words of the Bible are inspired by God or "God-breathed." If the Bible is the inspired Word of God, then it must be without error.

Often times, inspiration and illumination are confused. In order to understand more clearly the difference between the two, it would be good to examine the process of inspiration.

### 1. Revelation

The first step in the process of inspiration is *revelation*. Myer Pearlman has described revelation as the act of God by which He communicates new truth about Himself that man, otherwise, could not find out no matter how hard he searched. God has chosen to reveal Himself through two means.

First, He has done so through nature (Psalm 19; Romans 1:18-32). This is known as General Revelation. Though it is universal—to all men, everywhere—it is limited because it can reveal only limited truths about God, such as His power, wisdom and greatness. It cannot reveal other attributes, such as His love, joy, redemptive plan, purpose for man, etc.

The second form of revelation is called Special Revelation. This is God's revelation of Himself, man and His purposes, through the Scriptures. The product of this revelation is the Bible, God's Word.

### 2. Inspiration

*Inspiration* is the second step in the process. Inspiration is the means by which God works through human prophets and apostles, without destroying their individual personalities and styles, to produce divinely inspired Scripture. The Holy Spirit moves upon the human writers, directing and guiding their every word, so that what is produced is literally the "God-breathed," authoritative writing of Scripture.

> *All Scripture is given by inspiration of God, and is profitable for doctrine, for reproof, for correction, for instruction in righteousness, that the man of God may be complete, thoroughly equipped for every good work* (2 Timothy 3:16-17).

### 3. Illumination

The third is *illumination*. It is the process where God enlightens man's mind so that he can understand God's inspired Word. Illumination is available to all Christians, while inspiration is limited to the prophets and apostles God chose to be the human instruments He used to produce the Divinely Inspired Word of God.

These prophets and apostles were given inspiration in order to write the Word of God; they also had illumination but in some cases it was limited, as was the case with Daniel in writing the 70 weeks of Daniel or John in writing the Book of Revelation.

Paul explains this in 1 Corinthians 13:9-12:

> *For we know in part and we prophesy in part. But when that which is perfect has come, then that which is in part will be done away. When I was a child, I spoke as a child, I understood as a child, I thought as a child; but when I became a man, I put away childish things. For now we see in a mirror, dimly, but then face to face. Now I know in part, but then I shall know just as I also am known.*

As Christians, we pray before reading our Bibles that the Lord would open our hearts and minds to the truths of the Bible. What we are praying for is the illumination of God's Word. *Open my eyes, that I may see Wondrous things from Your law* (Psalm 119:18).

## C. The Verification of the Scriptures

Opinions alter, but truth certified by God can no more change than the God who uttered it.

—C.H. Spurgeon

How do we know the words of the Bible are truly the Words of God? Well, in the Old Testament, the writers themselves attribute the writing to God. We see the writers use the term *and God said*, or other similar terms over 2,600 times.

To further support the validity of the Old Testament teachings, Christ, Himself, quoted the Old Testament repeatedly. Examples of this are found in Matthew 5:18, 23:1-2, 26:54; John 10:35 and Luke 18:31-33, 24:25, 44. The Apostles also quoted the Old Testament in Romans 3:2; 2 Timothy 3:16; Hebrews 1:1 and 2 Peter 1:21 to list a few.

With the writers of the New Testament quoting the words of the Old Testament, we can see the agreement between the two sections of the Bible. The New Testament gives a clearer revelation of the Old Testament.

If we accept the evidence of the inspiration of the Old Testament, and the New Testament is in agreement with the Old, we can only conclude that it must also be inspired.

There are six evidences that verify the Scriptures. Three of them are *internal* and three of them are *external*. Some of the internal evidences we have touched on earlier, but they need to be repeated.

### 1. Internal

The first internal evidence is *the unity of the Bible*. The Old Testament was written over a period of 1000 years, and the New Testament was written over a period of about 60 years—in between the two, there was a 400 year period of silence. The Bible was written by over 40 writers, on three continents, over a period of 1500 years, and yet all the books are in complete unity and agreement.

The second internal evidence is *prophecy*. Throughout the Old Testament, we see prophecy of things to come, including the birth of the Savior. Not only was His birth prophesied, but the city where He would be born (Micah 5:2); that He would be born of a virgin (Isaiah 7:14); that He would be rejected (Isaiah 53:3); beaten (Isaiah 53:5); put on a cross (Psalm 22:16) and rise from the dead to redeem Israel (Psalm 130:8).

In the New Testament, we see the fulfillment of these prophecies (Romans 8:38). Today, we see the fulfillment of many other prophecies, such as the re-establishment of the country Israel, the current alignment of the Mid-Eastern countries against Israel, and Russia joining them in their stand.

The third internal evidence is the *authority and power of the Words of Scripture* (Romans 8:38). They are written with absolute conviction, without hesitations or second guesses. At no time do the writers indicate uncertainty in what they were writing. They knew the words were written with God's power and authority.

As I said earlier, there are six evidences to support the authority of the Bible. We have covered the three internal evidences, and now we will look at the three external evidences.

### 2.   External

First, *history* supports the words of the Bible. There are many historical books and scientific books that support facts written in the Bible. These facts were documented in the Bible long before these historical and scientific books were written. We have the Dead Sea Scrolls found in Qumran in 1947 and proven to be written between 200 B.C. and 100 A.D., some as early as 400 B.C. This archeological find demonstrated the unequaled accuracy of those copying the Old Testament Scriptures over a thousand year period.

Scientifically, the Bible, in Isaiah 40:22, revealed that the earth was round long before man discovered it: *It is He who sits above the circle of the earth, And its inhabitants are like grasshoppers, Who stretches out the heavens like a curtain, And spreads them out like a tent to dwell in.*

At one time, doctors would bleed their patients as a healing procedure. Often times, the patients would die from this process, not their illness. Today, science has determined that healthy blood is necessary for the health of the entire body. Our blood carries nutrients to every cell of our bodies. If the doctors had read their Bibles 120 years ago, they would have seen in Leviticus 17:11, 14, that God already told us our blood is important to our health, *For the life of the flesh is in the blood.*

In Ecclesiastes 1:6, the Word reveals the currents of the winds: *The wind goes toward the south, And turns around to the north; The wind whirls about continually, And comes again on its circuit.*

For those who worry about global warming and the water overtaking the land, God controls the boundaries of the water and the land. In Jeremiah 5:22, the LORD tells us:

> " 'Do you not fear Me?' says the LORD. 'Will you not tremble at My presence, Who have placed the sand as the bound of the sea, By a perpetual decree, that it cannot pass beyond it? And though its waves toss to and fro, Yet they cannot prevail; Though they roar, yet they cannot pass over it.' "

Second, the *authors* themselves are evidence of the Scriptures. Their lives were transformed by the words they wrote (James 1:21). In the New Testament, many of the writers gave firsthand accounts of Jesus and His life, and many of them suffered and gave their lives for what they believed and wrote. Paul was imprisoned in Rome for years before he was killed, and he never renounced the Lord, but evangelized everyone who came in contact with him.

Third, many in the world have tried to destroy the Word of God, but it has remained *indestructable*. In communist countries, like the former Soviet Union, Cuba and China, the Bible has been outlawed and burned, yet thousands in these countries have come to the Lord in spite of persecution. We see this today in many of the Muslim countries, with many converting to Christianity at the expense of their lives.

With all of the evidence supporting the Scriptures, it is clear that it is the inspired Word of God, and the Bible is inerrant. To say any part of the Bible is not true or accurate is to say the entire book is false. God is perfect and does not make mistakes (Titus 1:2; Hebrews 6:18). If we say He made an error in the Bible, then it cannot be inspired by Him.

## D. The Canonicity and Authority of the Scriptures

The word *canon* comes from the Greek *kanon*, meaning "a measuring rod or reed." It signifies a rule or a standard. Based upon this definition, the Canon of the Bible is comprised of the books considered worthy or that measured up to the standard in order to be included in the Holy Scriptures.

While a standard was established to determine the authenticity of the writings, it was not man who inspired the writings. They measured up to the standard because they were inspired by God.

> The various books possessed and exercised divine authority long before men ever made pronouncements to that effect. Ecclesiastical councils did not give the books their divine authority, but merely recognized that they both had it and exercised it.
>
> —Anonymous

## 1. Old Testament

The actual date for the closing of the Old Testament canon is subject to discussion among many Bible scholars. The Scriptures do not give us a closing date for the canon. What is important is that the Old Testament canon was complete at the time of Christ.

There are many instances throughout the Old Testament when a person recorded something for the people's remembrance. In Deuteronomy 31, we have what is believed to be the earliest writing of the Old Testament with Moses writing the Law and commanding the Levites to place it in the Ark of the Covenant.

Joshua followed the example set by Moses and wrote as he was inspired by God: *Then Joshua wrote these words in the Book of the Law of God. And he took a large stone, and set it up there under the oak that was by the sanctuary of the LORD* (Joshua 24:26).

Later, Samuel recorded events of his days and dedicated the record to the Lord in 1 Samuel 10:25: *Then Samuel explained to the people the behavior of royalty, and wrote it in a book and laid it up before the LORD.*

In Jeremiah 36:2, the LORD told the prophet to make a record for His people:

> *"Take a scroll of a book and write on it all the words that I have spoken to you against Israel, against Judah, and against all the nations, from the day I spoke to you, from the days of Josiah even to this day."*

In further support of the authority of the Old Testament canon, we see prophets, priests, kings and leaders consulting the words written by those who had gone before them:

> *In the first year of his reign I, Daniel, understood by the books the number of the years specified by the word of the LORD through Jeremiah the prophet, that He would accomplish seventy years in the desolations of Jerusalem* (Daniel 9:2).

*Now all the people gathered together as one man in the open square that was in front of the Water Gate; and they told Ezra the scribe to bring the Book of the Law of Moses, which the LORD had commanded Israel. So Ezra the priest brought the Law before the assembly of men and women and all who could hear with understanding on the first day of the seventh month. Then he read from it in the open square that was in front of the Water Gate from morning until midday, before the men and women and those who could understand; and the ears of all the people were attentive to the Book of the Law* (Nehemiah 8:1-3).

*Then Hilkiah the high priest said to Shaphan the scribe, "I have found the Book of the Law in the house of the LORD." And Hilkiah gave the book to Shaphan, and he read it* (2 Kings 22:8).

*The king went up to the house of the LORD with all the men of Judah, and with him all the inhabitants of Jerusalem; the priests and the prophets and all the people, both small and great. And he read in their hearing all the words of the Book of the Covenant which had been found in the house of the LORD* (2 Kings 23:2).

While no one is completely certain as to the exact time of the Old Testament canonicity, there is no doubt that it was completed before the time of Christ. Jesus, refering to the Old Testament said, *"You search the Scriptures, for in them you think you have eternal life; and these are they which testify of Me"* (John 5:39). Luke wrote: *And beginning at Moses and the Prophets, He* [Jesus] *expounded to them in all the Scriptures the things concerning Himself* (Luke 24:27). Jesus put His stamp of approval on the entire Old Testament Scriptures.

Jesus further confirms the Scriptures in Luke 11:51 . . . *from the blood of Abel to the blood of Zechariah who perished between the altar and the temple. Yes, I say to you, it shall be required of this generation.* Jesus is referencing the martyrs from Abel, in Genesis 4, to Zechariah, recorded in 2 Chronicles 24:20-21. In this verse, Jesus is validating the canonicity of the Hebrew Bible, which is the Old Testament from Genesis through 2 Chronicles, and that they were approved at the time of His walk on the earth.

Therefore, the Christian Bible, with 39 books in the Old Testament, is in complete agreement with the Hebrew Bible, which has 24 books. The variance in the number of books is because of how the Christian Bible divided some books. In the Hebrew Bible, the Minor Prophets—Hosea to Malachi—are one book, and 1 & 2 Samuel, 1 & 2 Kings and 1 & 2 Chronicles are each one book. Josephus, a trusted Jewish historian and Pharisee, also combined Ruth with Judges, Ezra with Nehemiah and Lamentations with Jeremiah. The actual words of the books have not been altered in the Christian Bible; the books have just been divided differently.

According to George L. Robinson in an article written for the *International Standard Bible Encyclopedia:*

> The books of the Law were recognized as canonical during the time of Ezra (444 B.C.); that the Prophets were recognized as such sometime later (around 200 B.C.) and that the Writings received authorization around 100 B.C.

While there may be open discussion as to the closing date of the canon for the Old Testament, the scriptural support from both the Old and New Testaments, along with historical writings, support the books chosen for canonicity.

## 2. The Apocrypha

The word *Apocrypha* refers to the 15 Apocryphal Books, which were added to the Old Testament and believed to be part of the sacred canon by many, particularly the Roman Catholic Church. They were included in the Greek translation of the Old Testament, the Septuagint (LXX) made between 280 B.C. and 180 B.C. Although Jerome translated the Apocrypha, he did not believe the books were inspired, so he did not include them in his original translation of the Latin Vulgate. However, these books were added to later versions of the Latin Vulgate, after his death.

However, they were later removed from the Protestant Bible for a number of reasons. To begin with, the Apocryphal Books were not a part of the Hebrew Bible, our Old Testament. Also, the Reformers wanted them removed because of their inconsistency with doctrine, i.e. praying for the dead and intercession by the saints. Last, while parts of almost all the Old Testament books are quoted or referenced in the New Testament, the Apocryphal Books are neither quoted nor referenced in the New Testament.

The 15 books, which are part of the Catholic Bible, but not the Protestant Bible, are: 1 Esdras, 2 Esdras, Tobit, Judith, the Rest of Esther, The Wisdom of Solomon, Ecclesiasticus, Baruch, the Epistle of Jeremiah, The Song of the Three Holy Children, The History of Susanna, Bel and the Dragon, The Prayer of Manasses, 1 Maccabees and 2 Maccabees.

## 3. New Testament

The New Testament was written during the last half of the first century A.D., so there is much more evidence available to trace the canonization of the 27 books. While the new Christian church had the Old Testament Scriptures for the foundation of their faith, the words of Jesus and the teachings of the Apostles were accepted as God's Word (John 3:34; 1 Thessalonians 2:13).

The Apostles were teaching based upon firsthand experience, having lived with Jesus during His ministry: *that which we have seen and heard we declare to you* (1 John 1:3); *For we . . . were eyewitnesses of His majesty* (2 Peter 1:16).

The early believers followed their teachings, *And they continued steadfastly in the apostles' doctrine and fellowship* (Acts 2:42).

The Epistles of Paul were important because of their spiritual value, addressing specific needs in the various churches. Because each letter addressed specific needs—exhorting, encouraging or clarifying a misunderstanding—all for the unity of the ministry, Paul charged them to share the letters with the other churches:

> *Now when this epistle is read among you, see that it is read also in the church of the Laodiceans, and that you likewise read the epistle from Laodicea* (Colossians 4:16).

> *I charge you by the Lord that this epistle be read to all the holy brethren* (1 Thessalonians 5:27).

Many of the other authors addressed their letters to multiple churches, further emphasizing the need to share the letters among the churches:

> *James, a bondservant of God and of the Lord Jesus Christ, To the twelve tribes which are scattered abroad: Greetings* (James 1:1).

> *Peter, an apostle of Jesus Christ, To the pilgrims of the Dispersion in Pontus, Galatia, Cappadocia, Asia, and Bithynia* (1 Peter 1:1).

> *What you see, write in a book and send it to the seven churches which are in Asia: to Ephesus, to Smyrna, to Pergamos, to Thyatira, to Sardis, to Philadelphia, and to Laodicea* (Revelation 1:11).

Prior to the final canonization of the 27 books of the New Testament by the third council of Carthage in 397, there were a number of books claiming to be inspired writings. Many of them were false teachings, and many were merely historical, not inspired, so they were not accepted in the final canon.

The decisions made concerning the books included in the New Testament were not done randomly. There were tests to determine whether a book fit the criteria. Dr. Duffield and Dr. Van Cleave give us a clear outline of the criteria for the books to be put in the canon, in their book, *Foundations of Pentecostal Theology:*

> The following principles were used to determine a book's place in the cannon:
> ### 1. Apostlicity
> Was the book written by an Apostle, or one who was closely associated with the Apostles? This question was especially important in relation to Mark, Luke, Acts and Hebrews; inasmuch as, Mark and Luke were not among the original twelve and the authorship of Hebrews was not known.
> ### 2. Spiritual Content
> Was the book being read in the churches and did its content prove a means of spiritual edification? This was a most practical test.
> ### 3. Doctrinal Soundness
> Were the contents of the book doctrinally sound? Any book containing heresy, or that which was contrary to the already accepted canonical books was rejected.
> ### 4. Usage
> Was the book universally recognized in the churches, and was it widely quoted by the Church Fathers?
> ### 5. Divine Inspiration
> Did it give true evidence of Divine inspiration? "This was the ultimate test; everything finally had to give way to it."

In the book of Hebrews, we are reminded of the importance of God's Word in our Christian walk:

> *For the word of God is living and powerful, and sharper than any two-edged sword, piercing even to the division of soul and spirit, and of joints and marrow, and is a discerner of the thoughts and intents of the heart* (Hebrews 4:12).

We need to read our Bibles and know God's Word as if our very lives depended on it. C. H. Spurgeon said it best: "Never defend a sword, just use it."

DOCTRINES

# Chapter 2
# DOCTRINE OF GOD
# THEOLOGY

## A. The Existence of God

## B. The Nature of God

Names of God

## C. The Attributes of God

Natural Attributes
1. The Omniscience of God
2. The Omnipotence of God
3. The Omnipresence of God
4. The Eternity of God

Moral Attributes
1. The Holiness of God
2. The Righteousness of God
3. The Mercy and Loving-Kindness of God
4. The Love of God

## D. The Trinity of God

## E. Creation

# DOCTRINE OF GOD
# THEOLOGY
Greek words: *theos* means "God," and
*ology* comes from *logos* which means "discourse" or "reason"

*Have you not known? Have you not heard? The everlasting God, the LORD, The Creator of the ends of the earth, Neither faints nor is weary. His understanding is unsearchable* (Isaiah 40:28).

## A. The Existence of God

The Bible never attempts to convince us or prove to us that God exists. Genesis 1:1 begins with, *In the beginning God. . . .* Every writer of the books of the Bible knew God, and therefore, was not inspired to provide proofs.

However, we attempt to prove the existence of God in order to assist those searching for Him and those that want evidence to support their faith. But make no mistake; our relationship with God comes down to our faith in Him.

There are three logical proofs for the existence of God: creation, design and human nature. First, we will look at creation. The universe had to have a beginning; it had to have been created. In order for it to be created, there had to be a Creator. Again, we read at the very beginning of the Bible in Genesis 1:1, *In the beginning God created the heavens and the earth.*

Second, we have the idea of design. The heavens and the earth were created in great detail and with great beauty. In order for design, detail and beauty to exist, there had to be a Designer, and not just any designer, but One of great intelligence, wisdom, power and vision.

Third and last, let's look at the nature of man. Man was created as a free moral agent, knowing the difference between right and wrong. God gave man a conscience, and it tells people whether their actions are morally right or morally wrong. In order for a person to innately have this conscience, there has to be a Lawgiver who has provided a standard or a moral compass—someone of great wisdom and intelligence—God.

## B. The Nature of God

*Westminster's Shorter Catechism* gives this definition of God: "God is a Spirit, infinite, eternal, and unchangeable in His being, wisdom, power, holiness, justice, goodness and truth."

God's nature is revealed in His name. In Exodus 3:13, Moses asked God who he should say sent him to the Israelites, and in verse 14, God responded, *And God said to Moses, "I AM WHO I AM."* He is the becoming One. He will be who we need in our time of need. There are many names of God, and they all reveal the nature of God.

**Names of God**
*Jehovah-Jireh:* The Lord will <u>Provide</u> (Genesis 22:13-14) Provedo
*Jehovah-Rapha:* The Lord that <u>Heals</u> (Exodus 15:26) Sanador
*Jehovah-Nissi:* The Lord our Banner (Exodus 17:8-15) Estandarte
*Jehovah-Shalom:* The Lord our Peace (Judges 6:24) Paz
*Jehovah-Ra-ah:* The Lord my Shepherd (Psalm 23:1) Pastor
*Jehovah-Tsidkenu:* The Lord our Righteousness
(Jeremiah 23:6) Justicia nuestra
*Jehovah Shammah:* The Lord is Present (Ezekiel 48:35) Ahi
*Jehovah Maccaddeshcem:* The Lord your Sanctifier
(Exodus 31:13) Santifica
*Elohim:* The plural form of *EL*, meaning "gods"(Genesis 1:1)
*El Shaddai:* God Almighty (Genesis 17:1) Todo Poderoso
*El Elyon:* The Most High God (Genesis 14:19) Altisimo
*El Olam:* The Everlasting God (Genesis 21:33) Eterno
*Yahweh (YHWH):* The All Becoming One (Exodus 3:14)

## C. The Attributes of God

God is eternal and infinite. We are finite, unable to fully comprehend the things of God, much less His full character. We recognize our limitations in comprehending God's character, when we read the writings of Paul. 1 Corinthians 1:25 says, *Because the foolishness of God is wiser than men, and the weakness of God is stronger than men.*

In addition, Romans 11:33 says, *How unsearchable are His judgments and His ways past finding out!*

So, we must enter into the study of the attributes of God with humility and reverence, knowing that we can only get a small glimpse of the greatness of God—those things which He reveals to us through His Word.

The attributes of God are traditionally split into two classifications: the *natural* and the *moral*. The natural attributes are His omniscience, His omnipotence, His omnipresence and His eternal existence. The moral attributes include His holiness, His righteousness, His mercy, His loving-kindness and His love.

### Natural Attributes
### 1. The Omniscience of God
This means that God knows all things. There is nothing in the universe that is a surprise to Him. He knows our thoughts and our hearts (Psalm 139:1-6). All things are known to Him—our biggest fears, darkest thoughts, deepest desires and highest aspirations—and yet knowing the good, the bad and the ugly, He loves us before we love Him. He often fulfills our greatest dreams before we even ask.

Scriptural evidence:

> *"Can you search out the deep things of God? Can you find out the limits of the Almighty? They are higher than heaven; what can you do? Deeper than Sheol; what can you know? Their measure is longer than the earth And broader than the sea"* (Job 11:7-9).

> *God is greater than our heart, and knows all things*
> (1 John 3:20).

## 2.   The Omnipotence of God

His power has no limits, and anything He wills He can bring to pass. The key to this statement is, *anything He wills*. God has power over everything, but does all things according to His will. When we come to God with our petitions, we must come in submission to Him, praying in His will, not ours. This is not to discourage you from lifting your petitions to God; remember, He can do all things.

Scriptural evidence:

> *I know that You can do everything, And that no purpose of Yours can be withheld from You* (Job 42:2).

> *But Jesus looked at them and said to them, "With men this is impossible, but with God all things are possible"* (Matthew 19:26).

## 3.   The Omnipresence of God

He is everywhere and in every place. It is a spiritual presence, not material. There is no place where we can hide from the presence of the Lord. Knowing He is everywhere and knows everything, why do we try to hide our sins and our thoughts from Him? This should not cause us to fear, but rather rejoice. God is with us in the midst of whatever trial or tribulation we are going through. He is sharing the joys and the pains of our lives and wants to celebrate with us and bring comfort to us.

Scriptural evidence:

> *And as soon as we heard these things, our hearts melted; neither did there remain any more courage in anyone because of you, for the LORD your God, He is God in heaven above and on earth beneath* (Joshua 2:11).

> *Where can I go from Your Spirit? Or where can I flee from Your presence? If I ascend into heaven, You are there; If I make my bed in hell, behold, You are there.*

*If I take the wings of the morning, And dwell in the uttermost parts of the sea, Even there Your hand shall lead me, And Your right hand shall hold me* (Psalm 139:7-10).

## 4. The Eternity of God

He is infinite, without a beginning, an ending or any limits. God is without constraints. He is eternal and unchanging. Why is this important to us? Because God does not change. His Word, His promises and His love for us do not change. God does not make decisions based on impulse, so His love for us is eternal and we can count on it.

Scriptural evidence:

*Even from everlasting to everlasting, You are God* (Psalm 90:2).

*Are You not from everlasting, O LORD my God, my Holy One?* (Habakkuk 1:12).

*For I am the LORD, I do not change* (Malachi 3:6).

## Moral Attributes
## 1. The Holiness of God

This is the most important moral attribute of God and the message of the entire Old Testament. God is holy and calls us to be holy. In Him is no evil; He does not make mistakes or judge unjustly. We can rest in the knowledge that He always has our best interest at heart and desires His best for us.

In the Old Testament, we saw that in order for the High Priest to enter the Holiest of Holies, he had to wear special garments, and he had to be sure to offer the required sacrifices before going in. If something happened to him while he was in there, the other priests had to pull him out by a rope tied to his leg. God's absolute holiness prevented them from entering into His presence.

Scriptural evidence:

> *For thus says the High and Lofty One Who inhabits eternity, whose name is Holy: "I dwell in the high and holy place* " (Isaiah 57:15).

> *But as He who called you is holy, you also be holy in all your conduct, because it is written, "Be holy, for I am holy"* (1 Peter 1:15-16).

## 2. The Righteousness of God

His righteousness is a manifestation of His holiness in His relationship with man. In His righteousness, God always does right. He is not moved to do things out of malice. We often think God is punishing us for some great sin we have committed, but it is just not in His nature to do anything out of malice. He is love and righteousness, and that is always what motivates Him.

Scriptural evidence:

> *The LORD is righteous in all His ways, Gracious in all His works* (Psalm 145:17).

> *Righteous are You, O LORD, when I plead with You* (Jeremiah 12:1).

> *If we confess our sins, He is faithful and just to forgive us our sins and to cleanse us from all unrighteousness* (1 John 1:9).

## 3. The Mercy and Loving-Kindness of God

He is kind, good and compassionate to all creation, both the saved and unsaved. His intention toward man is always for our welfare, never intending ill. Whether we are obedient or disobedient, God seeks to save us from the bondage of our sin.

Scriptural evidence:

> *The LORD is merciful and gracious, Slow to anger, and abounding in mercy* (Psalm 103:8).

> *For I know the thoughts that I think toward you, says the LORD, thoughts of peace and not of evil, to give you a future and a hope* (Jeremiah 29:11).

> *Therefore be merciful, just as your Father also is merciful* (Luke 6:36).

## 4. The Love of God

Christianity is the only religion that is based upon love, and that is because God is love. He is not just loving—He is the personification of love. Our relationship with God is based upon His love for us, not our love for Him.

Martin Luther expressed the importance of God's love for us when he said: "God does not love us because we are valuable, but we are valuable because God loves us."

The word *love* speaks of an unconditional love. This means there are no conditions that first have to be met in order for Him to love me. He loves me and I never have to do anything to earn it. 1 John 4:10 says, *In this is love, not that we loved God, but that He loved us and sent His Son to be the propitiation for our sins.*

Also, God demonstrated His love by sending His own Son to die for me. This gives me great assurance, because He was willing to give the greatest sacrifice in order to have a personal relationship with me for all eternity.

Scriptural evidence:

> *He who does not love does not know God, for God is love* (1 John 4:8).

> *God is love, and he who abides in love abides in God, and God in him* (1 John 4:16).

> *We love Him because He first loved us* (1 John 4:19).

## D. The Trinity of God

God exists eternally in three Persons: the Father, the Son, and the Holy Spirit. All are equal in power and divine perfection; all three are uncreated; and all three execute distinct and harmonious offices—creation, redemption and sanctification.

The Trinity is alluded to in the first verse of the Bible. Genesis 1:1 says, *In the beginning God.* The name used here for *God,* in Hebrew, is *Elohim,* the plural form for God. *El* is the singular word for God.

The Trinity of God is also seen at the baptism of Jesus in Matthew 3:16-17:

> *When He had been baptized, Jesus came up immediately from the water; and behold, the heavens were opened to Him, and He saw the Spirit of God descending like a dove and alighting upon Him. And suddenly a voice came from heaven, saying, "This is My beloved Son, in whom I am well pleased."*

We see the Son being baptized by John, the Holy Spirit descending as a dove, and the voice of the Father speaking, acknowledging His Son.

For many, the doctrine of the Trinity is very difficult to comprehend and apply to their Christian walk. I believe Donald Grey Barnhouse has the perfect explanation for belief in the Trinity of God: "The word *Trinity* is not found in the Bible, but the truth of this doctrine is in every part of the book."

## E. Creation

In Genesis 1:1, *In the beginning God created the heavens and the earth,* we see that the universe was created by the Word of God. God spoke it into existence in Genesis 1:3: *Then God said, "Let there be light"; and there was light.* The Hebrew word used for *created* is *bara,* which is always used in reference to divine creation or things produced that had no prior existence.

*By faith we understand that the worlds were framed by the word of God, so that the things which are seen were not made of things which are visible* (Hebrews 11:3).

*In the beginning was the Word, and the Word was with God, and the Word was God. He was in the beginning with God. All things were made through Him, and without Him nothing was made that was made* (John 1:1-3).

Keep in mind; we do not study theology to only know about God, but to know Him personally (John 17:3). God is just waiting to show Himself to those who seek Him (2 Chronicles 16:9). He is not a respecter of persons (Acts 10:34) and He has a special heart for those in need (Psalm 138:6; Luke 4:18-19).

# CHAPTER 3

# DOCTRINE OF JESUS CHRIST
## CHRISTOLOGY

## A. The Nature of Jesus Christ

**Six titles that encompass His nature**
1. Son of God
2. The Word
3. Lord
4. Son of Man
5. The Christ
6. Son of David
7. Jesus

## B. The Offices of Jesus Christ

## C. The Work of Jesus Christ
1. Christ's Death
2. Christ's Resurrection
   Eyewitness Accounts
   Physical Proofs
3. Christ's Ascension into Heaven

## D. Atonement through Jesus Christ
**Results of Atonement**
1. Forgiveness of Our Sins
2. Freedom from Our Sins
3. Victorious Living
4. Eternal Life

## Doctrine of Jesus Christ
# CHRISTOLOGY
Greek words: *Christos* means "anointed," and *ology*, "knowledge"

*Therefore I will divide Him a portion with the great, And He shall divide the spoil with the strong, Because He poured out His soul unto death, And He was numbered with the transgressors, And He bore the sin of many, And made intercession for the transgressors* (Isaiah 53:12).

*Jesus Christ is the same yesterday, today, and forever* (Hebrews 13:8).

## A. The Nature of Jesus Christ
The nature of Christ is revealed in His titles, names the Bible uses in reference to Him. The following are six titles or names that encompass His nature:

### 1. The Son of God
*The Son of God* reveals His deity. He is *the* Son of God, not *a* son of God, as the angels and men are called. In Matthew 4:3-6, Satan acknowledges the deity of Christ as he called Him Son of God twice. The people recognize Him as the Son of God in Matthew 14:33, *Then those who were in the boat came and worshiped Him, saying, "Truly You are the Son of God."*

### 2. The Word
*The Word* reveals that Jesus is eternal—pre-existing. In John 1:1-2, we see that He was with God in the beginning: *In the beginning was the Word, and the Word was with God, and the Word was God. He was in the beginning with God.*

A man's words define his ideas and thoughts. Jesus not only delivers the message of God, but He *is* God's message. He reveals God's wisdom, knowledge, power and intelligence through the Word.

### 3.  Lord

*Lord* reveals the sovereignty, deity and exaltation of Christ. The title *Lord* was recognized by both the Jews and the Gentiles as a sign of divinity, and we see it used throughout the Book of Acts and the Epistles, as Paul and the other apostles recognize the act of sacrifice Christ made on the cross. He was born divine, and He is acknowledged as *Lord* throughout the gospels (Matthew 17:4; John 11:21), but He earned the title *Lord Jesus* at the cross. The first time we see the title *Lord Jesus* is in Luke 24:3: *Then they went in and did not find the body of the Lord Jesus.*

### 4.  Son of Man

The *Son of Man* reveals His humanity. While His title of deity makes known His nature as God's Son, this title, which He gave Himself, also exposes His human nature and qualities, which include human weakness and infirmities. Christ experienced hunger (Matthew 4:2), thirst (John 19:28), pain (Matthew 27:26), humility (Matthew 27:29), agony (Luke 22:44) and sadness (John 11:35). His divine nature did not protect Him from these very human sufferings.

### 5.  The Christ

The *Christ* is His official title and mission. *Christ* is the Greek word for His Hebrew title of *Messiah*, which means "the Anointed One." He came as the Anointed One to fulfill the promise in the Old Testament of a Messiah— a Savior.

In Matthew 1:1, 16, 17 we find the first references to Jesus as the Christ in the lineage:

*The book of the genealogy of Jesus Christ, the Son of David, the Son of Abraham* (Matthew 1:1).

*And Jacob begot Joseph the husband of Mary, of whom was born Jesus who is called Christ* (Matthew 1:16).

*So all the generations from Abraham to David are fourteen generations, from David until the captivity in Babylon are fourteen generations, and from the captivity in Babylon until the Christ are fourteen generations* (Matthew 1:17).

The first reference to Jesus as the Messiah is found in John 1:41: *He first found his own brother Simon, and said to him, "We have found the Messiah" (which is translated, the Christ).*

## 6. Son of David

The *Son of David* speaks of His royal lineage. This title is equal to the title of Messiah, because one of the requirements of the Messiah is that He be born of the line of David. In Matthew 1 and Luke 3, we trace the lineage of Jesus from Abraham, through David to Joseph and Mary, His earthly parents.

The first reference to Christ as the *Son of David* is found in Matthew 1:1: *The book of the genealogy of Jesus Christ, the Son of David, the Son of Abraham.*

## 7. Jesus

His name *Jesus* speaks of His saving work. God sent His Only Begotten Son to save the world from their sins. In Matthew 1:21, an angel of the Lord appears to Joseph and tells him of Mary's pregnancy. He also gives him the name of the Child and speaks of His mission: *And she will bring forth a Son, and you shall call His name JESUS, for He will save His people from their sins.*

## B. The Offices of Jesus Christ

In the Old Testament, God used men to speak to His people. There were prophets, priests, kings and judges—all human vessels used by the Lord. In the New Testament, God sent His Son to fulfill all the Old Testament offices (Luke 11:32). Jesus was a *Prophet* speaking God's Word (John 12:49-50).

As *Priest*, Jesus is the *Mediator* between God and man, and there is no other, as Paul tells his young apprentice, *For there is one God and one Mediator between God and men, the Man Christ Jesus* (1 Timothy 2:5).

Jesus is also *King*. He came to announce the coming Kingdom: *From that time Jesus began to preach and to say, "Repent, for the kingdom of heaven is at hand"* (Matthew 4:17). He also came to forgive sin: *Then He said to her, "Your sins are forgiven"* (Luke 7:48).

Ultimately, Christ will fulfill the office of *Judge*. In John 5:22, we see that Christ will judge all men: *For the Father judges no one, but has committed all judgment to the Son.*

## C. The Work of Jesus Christ

While Christ walked among men, He performed many works— many miracles—but He was sent by the Father to die on the cross for the sins of the world. However, dying could not fully complete this work. His work was threefold: He had to *die* for our sins, *rise* from the dead to give us new life and *ascend* to heaven to become our Intercessor. Everything He did was for you and me.

### 1. Christ's Death

First, *Christ died* for our sins: *And you know that He was manifested to take away our sins, and in Him there is no sin* (1 John 3:5).

The importance of His death cannot be stressed more. In the Old Testament, the Jews were required to provide sacrifices for their sins. The blood of the animals provided a temporary covering for their sin, but not complete forgiveness.

When Christ died on the cross, He provided complete and total forgiveness for our sins—not only the sins we had committed, but those sins we have yet to commit. According to Romans 7:14, I was a slave to my sins: *For we know that the law is spiritual, but I am carnal, sold under sin.*

Through Christ's death on the cross, He paid the ransom for my soul: *just as the Son of Man did not come to be served, but to serve, and to give His life a ransom for many* (Matthew 20:28).

## 2.   Christ's Resurrection

Then, *Christ rose from the dead.* The whole of Christianity rests upon the resurrection of Christ. Without this miracle, Christians have no hope, and Christianity is a dead religion based on man and not God. Through the resurrection, we know that Christ is all He claimed to be, the Son of God, and one day we will be with Him:

> *Jesus Christ our Lord . . . declared to be the Son of God with power according to the Spirit of holiness, by the resurrection from the dead* (Romans 1:3-4).

> *For if we believe that Jesus died and rose again, even so God will bring with Him those who sleep in Jesus* (1 Thessalonians 4:14).

> *Knowing that He who raised up the Lord Jesus will also raise us up with Jesus, and will present us with you* (2 Corinthians 4:14).

The resurrection is not something of myths or conjecture. There are proofs and evidence throughout the Bible to support the cornerstone of Christianity.

### Eyewitness Accounts of the Resurrection of Christ

In these appearances of Christ after the resurrection, the witnesses saw, heard or touched Jesus. They also bore evidence of the empty tomb, linen clothes or the scars.

    a.  Seen by Mary and Mary Magdalene - Matthew 28:1-10

    b.  Seen by two on the road to Emmaus - Luke 24:13-16

    c.  Seen by Apostles - Matthew 28:16-17; John 20:19-31

    d.  Seen by five hundred - 1 Corinthians 15:6

    e.  Seen by Paul - Acts 9:1-9

### Physical Proofs of the Resurrection

    a.  His empty tomb - Matthew 28:6-15

    b.  His linen clothes - Luke 24:12; John 20:6-10

    c.  He ate food - Luke 24:30; Luke 24:41-43; John 21:12-15

    d.  He bore the scars - Luke 24:39-40; John 20:27

    e.  He was touched and handled - Matthew 28:9; Luke 24:39; 1 John 1:1

    f.  He was flesh and bones - Luke 24:39

### 3.  Christ's Ascension into Heaven

Then, *Jesus ascended* to heaven to sit at the right hand of the Father to be our defense: *Who is he who condemns? It is Christ who died, and furthermore is also risen, who is even at the right hand of God, who also makes intercession for us* (Romans 8:34).

Christ not only died once and for all for our sins, but He intercedes on our behalf. His work did not die on the cross, but is a living thing, because He has power and authority at the throne of God: *Therefore He is also able to save to the uttermost those who come to God through Him, since He always lives to make intercession for them* (Hebrews 7:25).

## D. Atonement through Jesus Christ

What is atonement? *The Encarta Dictionary* lists two definitions for the word *atonement*: 1. Making of amends—the making of reparation for a sin or a mistake; 2. Reconciliation between God and people—in Christian belief, the reconciliation between God and people brought about by the death of Jesus Christ.

In Hebrew, the word for *atonement* means "to cover." The covering is not just of the sin, but of the sinner.

Why is atonement necessary? The need for atonement is found in two basic facts—God's holiness and man's sinfulness. God is holy, and we cannot approach Him in our sinful nature (Habakkuk 1:12). It is only through the atoning work of Jesus Christ that we are able to enter into fellowship with God. Through Christ, we are made "at-one-ment" with God. His righteousness has been imputed to us:

> *And be found in Him, not having my* [Paul's] *own righteousness, which is from the law, but that which is through faith in Christ, the righteousness which is from God by faith* (Philippians 3:9).

> *By that will* [of God] *we have been sanctified through the offering of the body of Jesus Christ once for all* (Hebrews 10:10).

Through atonement, we are redeemed or liberated from captivity: *In Him we have redemption through His blood, the forgiveness of sins, according to the riches of His grace which He made to abound toward us in all wisdom and prudence* (Ephesians 1:7-8).

Unlike the animal sacrifices of the Old Testament, which only temporarily covered sin, through the blood of Christ we are delivered or set free from sin: *Not with the blood of goats and calves, but with His own blood He entered the Most Holy Place once for all, having obtained eternal redemption* (Hebrews 9:12).

### Results of Atonement
1.  Forgiveness of our sins: *In Him we have redemption through His blood, the forgiveness of sins, according to the riches of His grace* (Ephesians 1:7).

2.  Freedom from our sins: *Therefore if the Son makes you free, you shall be free indeed* (John 8:36).

3.  Victorious living: *I have been crucified with Christ; it is no longer I who live, but Christ lives in me; and the life which I now live in the flesh I live by faith in the Son of God, who loved me and gave Himself for me* (Galatians 2:20).

4.  Eternal life: *That whoever believes in Him should not perish but have eternal life* (John 3:15).

# Chapter 4

# DOCTRINE OF THE HOLY SPIRIT
## PNEUMATOLOGY

## A. The Nature of the Holy Spirit

Names of the Holy Spirit
1. Spirit of God
2. Spirit of Christ
3. Comforter
4. Holy Spirit
5. Holy Spirit of Promise
6. Spirit of Truth
7. Spirit of Grace and Supplication
8. Spirit of Life
9. Spirit of Adoption

Symbols of the Holy Spirit
1. Fire
2. Wind
3. Water
4. Seal
5. Oil
6. Dove

## B. The Spirit in the Old Testament

## C. The Spirit in the Life and Ministry of Jesus Christ

## D. The Spirit in Human Experience

1. The With Experience
2. The In Experience
3. The Upon Experience

## E. The Spirit in the Church

## F. The Fruit of the Spirit

## G. The Gifts of the Spirit

Three Categories of Spiritual Gifts
1. Supernatural Knowledge
2. Supernatural Action
3. Supernatural Speaking

# DOCTRINE OF THE HOLY SPIRIT
# PNEUMATOLOGY

Greek words: *pneuma* means "spirit," *ology*, "knowledge"

*The Spirit of the Lord GOD is upon Me, Because the LORD has anointed Me To preach good tidings to the poor; He has sent Me to heal the brokenhearted, To proclaim liberty to the captives, And the opening of the prison to those who are bound* (Isaiah 61:1).

*The Spirit of the LORD shall rest upon Him, The Spirit of wisdom and understanding, The Spirit of counsel and might, The Spirit of knowledge and of the fear of the LORD* (Isaiah 11:2).

## A. The Nature of the Holy Spirit

The Holy Spirit is the third person of the Trinity, and, as with God the Father and Jesus Christ, His nature is revealed in the many names given to Him and symbols used to represent Him throughout the Scriptures.

### Names of the Holy Spirit

1. **Spirit of God**

   *The earth was without form, and void; and darkness was on the face of the deep. And the Spirit of God was hovering over the face of the waters* (Genesis 1:2).

2. **Spirit of Christ**

   *But you are not in the flesh but in the Spirit, if indeed the Spirit of God dwells in you. Now if anyone does not have the Spirit of Christ, he is not His* (Romans 8:9).

3. **Comforter**

   *But the Helper, [Comforter], the Holy Spirit, whom the Father will send in My name, He will teach you all things, and bring to your remembrance all things that I said to you* (John 14:26).

4. **Holy Spirit**

   *"For David himself said by the Holy Spirit: 'The LORD said to my Lord, "Sit at My right hand, Till I make Your enemies Your footstool" ' "* (Mark 12:36).

5. **Holy Spirit of Promise**

   *In Him you also trusted, after you heard the word of truth, the gospel of your salvation; in whom also, having believed, you were sealed with the Holy Spirit of promise, who is the guarantee of our inheritance until the redemption of the purchased possession, to the praise of His glory* (Ephesians 1:13-14).

6. **Spirit of Truth**

   *However, when He, the Spirit of truth, has come, He will guide you into all truth; for He will not speak on His own authority, but whatever He hears He will speak; and He will tell you things to come* (John 16:13).

7. **Spirit of Grace and Supplication**

   *And I will pour on the house of David and on the inhabitants of Jerusalem the Spirit of grace and supplication; then they will look on Me whom they pierced* (Zechariah 12:10).

8. **Spirit of Life**

   *For the law of the Spirit of life in Christ Jesus has made me free from the law of sin and death* (Romans 8:2).

9.  Spirit of Adoption
*For you did not receive the spirit of bondage again to fear, but you received the Spirit of adoption by whom we cry out, "Abba, Father"* (Romans 8:15).

## Symbols of the Holy Spirit

1.  **Fire:** represents purification and illumination (Isaiah 4:4; Matthew 3:11; Acts 2:3).

The work of the silversmith is a perfect example of the Holy Spirit working as fire in the believer's life.  In order to purify the silver before it can be made into a fine piece of jewelry or a utensil, the silversmith turns up the fire, heating the silver until the dross, or impurities, rise to the top.  As he skims the impurities from the top, he can begin to see his image in the bubbling cauldron.  Once he can see his image clearly, he knows the silver is pure, without dross.  God is refining us, so that He can see His very image in us.

2.  **Wind:** represents the regenerating work of the Holy Spirit (Ezekiel 37:7-10; John 3:5-8; Acts 2:1-2).

The Spirit as the wind is the breath of God, breathing new life into man when he is dead in his sins. It also represents the coming of the Holy Spirit to dwell with man.

3.  **Water:** represents living water, cleansing away sin (John 3:5, 4:14, 7:38-39).

Once we receive Christ, the Holy Spirit flows through us, satisfying our thirst for God and filling us with living water unto life everlasting.

4.  **Seal:** represents ownership (John 6:27; Ephesians 1:13-14; 4:30; 2 Corinthians 1:22; 2 Timothy 2:19).

During the days of royal monarchies, the king and his court each had signet rings that represented their families.  When they wrote a letter or note, they would seal it with hot wax and then press their signet ring into the wax. This way, the recipient of the letter knew from the unbroken seal, that the letter was truly from the person and not a forgery. We are sealed by the Holy Spirit, indicating that we are truly owned by God.

5. **Oil**: represents life, transformation and consecration (1 Samuel 16:13; Isaiah 61:1; Mark 14:3-8; Acts 10:38; 2 Corinthians 1:21; 1 John 2:20).

In the Bible, oil was used to anoint those who God would set apart to be leaders, as with Saul and David, or as a preparation for burial, as with Jesus. The oil was used to indicate a transformed life. Today, we use oil to anoint people and pray for them when they are sick or being consecrated to the service of the Lord (Mark 6:13; James 5:14).

6. **Dove**: represents peace, purity and innocence (Genesis 8:11; Matthew 3:16; Luke 3:21-22; John 1:32).

The dove is used as a symbol in weddings, indicating the purity, peace and innocence that should be represented. Solomon (a type of Christ), refers to the Shulamite (a type of the Church), His true love, as a dove. She refers to Him as having eyes like doves (Song of Solomon 5:12, 6:9). The dove is a symbol of the purity and perfection they see in each other. In the New Testament, the Holy Spirit, in the form of a gentle dove, descended upon Jesus at His baptism.

## B. The Spirit in the Old Testament

While the name *Holy Spirit* is found more often in the New Testament than in the Old Testament, the third person of the Trinity, the Holy Spirit, was a vital presence in the Old Testament.

At the very beginning, in Genesis, we see Him as the Creative Spirit. He was with God the Father and Jesus at the creation of the world in Genesis 1:2: *The earth was without form, and void; and darkness was on the face of the deep. And the Spirit of God was hovering over the face of the waters.*

He was also with them at the creation of man. The triune God is seen in the words *Us* and *Our* in Genesis 1:26:

> *Then God said, "Let Us make man in Our image, according to Our likeness; let them have dominion over the fish of the sea, over the birds of the air, and over the cattle, over all the earth and over every creeping thing that creeps on the earth."*

God made man in order to establish a society governed by God, which was led by the Spirit of God. It is through the Holy Spirit, man would be inspired in word and in deed.

In Numbers 11:17, we see how the Lord poured out His Spirit on those who were to serve Him:

> *Then I will come down and talk with you there. I will take of the Spirit that is upon you and will put the same upon them; and they shall bear the burden of the people with you, that you may not bear it yourself alone.*

When a prophet spoke the Words of the LORD in the Old Testament, he would begin with phrases such as, *Thus says the LORD*. In Exodus 5:1, the LORD speaks through Moses to Pharaoh: *Afterward Moses and Aaron went in and told Pharaoh, "Thus says the LORD God of Israel: 'Let My people go, that they may hold a feast to Me in the wilderness.' "*

As prophets and teachers, using the phrase *Thus says the LORD* held tremendous responsibility. Once those words were spoken, you were representing the LORD and the message He had given through His Spirit. For this reason, we see the warning to false prophets in Ezekiel 13:1-3:

> *And the Word of the LORD came to me, saying, "Son of man, prophesy against the prophets of Israel who prophesy, and say to those who prophesy out of their own heart, 'Hear the word of the LORD!' " Thus says the Lord GOD: "Woe to the foolish prophets, who follow their own spirit and have seen nothing!"*

The Holy Spirit not only inspired man, but instructed him in moral conduct and regenerated his spirit. We see God's instruction through the Holy Spirit in Nehemiah 9:20: *You also gave Your good Spirit to instruct them, And did not withhold Your manna from their mouth, And gave them water for their thirst.* In Psalm 51:11-12, David sought the regenerating power of the Holy Spirit: *Do not cast me away from Your presence, And do not take Your Holy Spirit from me. Restore to me the joy of Your salvation, And uphold me by Your generous Spirit.*

So, as you can see scripturally, the Holy Spirit was an active and essential participant in the Old Testament.

## C. The Spirit in the Life and Ministry of Jesus Christ

The Holy Spirit worked with, in, and through Jesus Christ throughout His ministry and was present at every crucial event in His life. He was with the Father and Son at the very beginning of creation, and He was with Christ at His conception.

It was through the Holy Spirit that Mary conceived the Son of God in Matthew 1:20:

> *But while he thought about these things, behold, an angel of the Lord appeared to him in a dream, saying, "Joseph, son of David, do not be afraid to take to you Mary your wife, for that which is conceived in her is of the Holy Spirit."*

With Christ's conception came the knowledge that God was ready to fulfill His promise to pour out His Spirit on man.

After the birth, we see Him at Christ's baptism in Luke 3:22: *And the Holy Spirit descended in bodily form like a dove upon Him, and a voice came from heaven which said, "You are My beloved Son; in You I am well pleased."*

During His ministry, the Holy Spirit was with Him when He was tempted by Satan in Mark 1:12: *Immediately the Spirit drove Him into the wilderness.*

Christ speaks of His anointing with the Holy Spirit in Luke 4:18:

> *The Spirit of the LORD is upon Me, Because He has anointed Me To preach the gospel to the poor; He has sent Me to heal the brokenhearted, To proclaim liberty to the captives And recovery of sight to the blind, To set at liberty those who are oppressed.*

It was the Holy Spirit that strengthened and enabled Christ to do the work He was called to at the cross: *who through the eternal Spirit offered Himself without spot to God* (Hebrews 9:14).

Following the crucifixion, the Holy Spirit was with Christ at the resurrection: *and was declared to be the Son of God with power according to the Spirit of holiness, by the resurrection from the dead* (Romans 1:4).

After the resurrection, we see a foretaste of the promise of God to pour out His Spirit upon man and write His Law on our hearts: *And when He had said this, He breathed on them, and said to them, "Receive the Holy Spirit"* (John 20:22).

This could only happen in fullness after Christ ascended into heaven with God the Father: *Therefore being exalted to the right hand of God, and having received from the Father the promise of the Holy Spirit, He poured out this which you now see and hear* (Acts 2:33).

From conception to the resurrection, the Holy Spirit was intimately connected to Christ's life and ministry. It was through the anointing of the Holy Spirit upon the Lord Jesus Christ that we see the fulfillment of God's promise to pour out His Spirit on all flesh.

## D. The Spirit in Human Experience

The Holy Spirit is our Helper. There are three ways in which we can potentially experience the Holy Spirit in our lives.

### 1. The With Experience

The first can be referred to as the *with* experience. This speaks of the Holy Spirit coming alongside of unbelievers to convict them of their sins and to help convince them to come to the LORD. Today, in the world, the Holy Spirit is actively working alongside each unbeliever in order to bring them to Christ (John 16:7-8).

### 2. The In Experience

The second is known as the *in* experience, which refers to the Holy Spirit dwelling in believers when they accept Jesus as Lord and Savior (1 Corinthians 6:19). These first two, the *in* and the *with* experiences are mentioned in John 14:16-17:

> *And I will pray the Father, and He will give you another Helper, that He may abide with you forever; the Spirit of truth, whom the world cannot receive, because it neither sees Him nor knows Him; but you know Him, for He dwells with you and will be in you.*

### 3. The Upon Experience

The third aspect is the *upon* experience that signifies the empowering of the believer for Christian service. In doing so, the power of God's Spirit will flow through us and touch the lives of those around us.

Jesus describes this outpouring of the Holy Spirit in John 7:38: *He who believes in Me, as the Scripture has said, out of his heart will flow rivers of living water.* The reference to the *upon* experience is found in Acts 1:8, which says, *But you shall receive power when the Holy Spirit has come upon you.* This act of the Holy Spirit empowering the believer is what is known as the Baptism with the Holy Spirit or the infilling of the Holy Spirit.

The evidence of being filled with the Spirit is love (1 Corinthians 13).

## E. The Spirit in the Church

As mentioned previously, the Holy Spirit was given to the church after the death and resurrection of Jesus Christ. We are now living in the days of the Holy Spirit when He is available to all who are believers in Jesus Christ and have accepted Him as Lord and Savior. He empowers the church to fulfill the great commission given by Jesus Christ in Acts 1:8:

> *But you shall receive power when the Holy Spirit has come upon you; and you shall be witnesses to Me in Jerusalem, and in all Judea and Samaria, and to the end of the earth.*

> *Then there appeared to them divided tongues, as of fire, and one sat upon each of them. And they were all filled with the Holy Spirit and began to speak with other tongues, as the Spirit gave them utterance* (Acts 2:3-4).

During this time, known as the Church Age, the Holy Spirit is the Helper and Comforter to the church. It is by His power that a person is saved, not the work of any man or message of man:

> *For our gospel did not come to you in word only, but also in power, and in the Holy Spirit and in much assurance, as you know what kind of men we were among you for your sake. And you became followers of us and of the Lord, having received the word in much affliction, with joy of the Holy Spirit* (1 Thessalonians 1:5-6).

Through the power of the Holy Spirit, the body of Christ grows as people are saved and added to the church: *And the Lord added to the church daily those who were being saved* (Acts 2:47).

The present work of the Holy Spirit in the church will end when the church is taken out of this world in the Rapture (1 Thessalonians 4:17), and the Tribulation begins on this earth

(Matthew 24:21). That is not to say the work of the Spirit will cease, but, just as Jesus went to be with the Father, the Holy Spirit will depart, along with the believers, at the end of the Church Age. For it is the Holy Spirit in the church that restrains the coming of the Antichrist: *For the mystery of lawlessness is already at work; only He* [the Holy Spirit] *who now restrains will do so until He is taken out of the way* (2 Thessalonians 2:7).

It will be a time as in the Old Testament, when the Holy Spirit came upon the saints momentarily, but did not dwell in them. There is no evidence of the indwelling of the Holy Spirit in the Old Testament or within the Tribulation saints. However, there will be some who are empowered by the Holy Spirit to witness during the Tribulation (Revelation 11:3).

We do not know the day or the hour the church and the Holy Spirit will depart from this world, but we do know that it will occur when the church is complete:

> *For I do not desire, brethren, that you should be ignorant of this mystery, lest you should be wise in your own opinion, that blindness in part has happened to Israel until the fullness of the Gentiles has come in* (Romans 11:25).

## F.  The Fruit of the Spirit

The Fruit of the Spirit is the manifestation of the indwelling of the Holy Spirit in our Christian walk. While the gifts of the Spirit are what He imparts to us, the Fruit of the Spirit is His character that is produced and grows in us through His work in our lives, as we yield to Him.

These spiritual characteristics are often completely foreign to our fleshly characteristics. In Galatians 5:19-23, Paul contrasts the Fruit of the Spirit with the long list of the works of our flesh:

> *Now the works of the flesh are evident, which are: adultery, fornication, uncleanness, lewdness, idolatry, sorcery, hatred, contentions, jealousies, outbursts of wrath, selfish ambitions,*

*dissensions, heresies, envy, murders, drunkenness, revelries, and the like; of which I tell you beforehand, just as I also told you in time past, that those who practice such things will not inherit the kingdom of God. But the fruit of the Spirit is love, joy, peace, longsuffering, kindness, goodness, faithfulness, gentleness, self-control. Against such there is no law.*

In verses 24 and 25, he goes on to explain that we are to yield to the work of the Spirit in us instead of yielding to our flesh: *And those who are Christ's have crucified the flesh with its passions and desires. If we live in the Spirit, let us also walk in the Spirit.*

So, we must crucify the flesh, or put off the old man, in order to live according to the Spirit.

If we do not yield to the Holy Spirit, then how will people know we are children of God? How can we say we are Christians if we choose to walk in our flesh instead of in His light? Let us then walk in the Spirit:

*For you were once darkness, but now you are light in the Lord. Walk as children of light (for the fruit of the Spirit is in all goodness, righteousness, and truth), finding out what is acceptable to the Lord* (Ephesians 5:8-10).

## G. The Gifts of the Spirit

The Gifts of the Spirit are given to believers for the building up of the church, the equipping of the saints and sharing the good news of Jesus Christ with unbelievers. Like the talents Jesus speaks of in Matthew 25, our gifts are not to be hidden, unused or hoarded for ourselves, but put to good use in building the Kingdom.

To better understand the gifts, they can be divided into three categories:

1. **Supernatural Knowledge**: word of wisdom, word of knowledge, discernment and administration.

2. **Supernatural Action**: love, ministry, giving, leadership, showing mercy, faith, healing, miracles and helps.

3. **Supernatural Speaking**: prophecy, teaching, exhortation, apostle, evangelism, pastor, speaking in tongues and interpretation of tongues.

Paul lists the diverse gifts of the Holy Spirit in his letters to the Romans, the Ephesians and the Corinthians and explains that, in their diversity, they are all of the same Spirit and given according to His will, not ours:

> *For as we have many members in one body, but all the members do not have the same function, so we, being many, are one body in Christ, and individually members of one another. Having then gifts differing according to the grace that is given to us, let us use them: if prophecy, let us prophesy in proportion to our faith; or ministry, let us use it in our ministering; he who teaches, in teaching; he who exhorts, in exhortation; he who gives, with liberality; he who leads, with diligence; he who shows mercy, with cheerfulness* (Romans 12:4-8).

> *And He Himself gave some to be apostles, some prophets, some evangelists, and some pastors and teachers, for the equipping of the saints for the work of ministry, for the edifying of the body of Christ* (Ephesians 4:11-12).

> *But the manifestation of the Spirit is given to each one for the profit of all: for to one is given the word of wisdom through the Spirit, to another the word of knowledge through the same Spirit, to another faith by the same Spirit, to another gifts of healings by the same Spirit, to another the working of miracles, to another prophecy, to another discerning of spirits, to another different kinds of tongues, to another the interpretation of tongues. But one and the same Spirit works all these things, distributing to each one individually as He wills* (1 Corinthians 12:7-11).

In 1 Corinthians, Paul goes on to explain, since the Spirit distributes gifts according to His will, we should never be jealous of the gifts of others, but seek how God would have us use the gift or gifts that have been given to each of us individually:

> *And God has appointed these in the church: first apostles, second prophets, third teachers, after that miracles, then gifts of healings, helps, administrations, varieties of tongues. Are all apostles? Are all prophets? Are all teachers? Are all workers of miracles? Do all have gifts of healings? Do all speak with tongues? Do all interpret? But earnestly desire the best gifts. And yet I show you a more excellent way* (1 Corinthians 12:28-31).

The one thing we must keep in mind when looking at our gifts and the gifts of others is that everything is temporal—but for a short time. *But whether there are prophecies, they will fail; whether there are tongues, they will cease; whether there is knowledge, it will vanish away* (1 Corinthians 13:8).

While many denominations put a strong emphasis on the gift of speaking in tongues as evidence of the infilling of the Holy Spirit, that is not what the Bible teaches. As a matter of fact, in 1 Corinthians 13:1, Paul makes it perfectly clear that this is not the most important gift: *Though I speak with the tongues of men and of angels, but have not love, I have become sounding brass or a clanging cymbal.*

Many people receive the gift of tongues when they are filled with the Holy Spirit, but many do not. This is a gift for the edification of oneself, not the Body of Christ. Paul goes on in 1 Corinthians 14:3-4, to tell us that the gift of prophecy is greater than tongues, because it edifies the church: *But he who prophesies speaks edification and exhortation and comfort to men. He who speaks in a tongue edifies himself, but he who prophesies edifies the Church.*

There is a time and a place for speaking in tongues. It should be done in your private prayer time or in a prayer service where there are those that have the gift of interpretation. Our God is a God of order (1 Corinthians 14:40).

In a group, do not speak in tongues unless there is an interpreter:

> *How is it then, brethren? Whenever you come together, each of you has a psalm, has a teaching, has a tongue, has a revelation, has an interpretation. Let all things be done for edification. If anyone speaks in a tongue, let there be two or at the most three, each in turn, and let one interpret. But if there is no interpreter, let him keep silent in church, and let him speak to himself and to God* (1 Corinthians 14:26-27).

The Bible lists 21 gifts of the Holy Spirit. If you would like to learn more about them, read 1 Corinthians 12-14. While there are many gifts, Paul tells us in 1 Corinthians 13:13 that the greatest manifestation of the Holy Spirit is love. Without love the gifts are meaningless. *And now abide faith, hope, love, these three; but the greatest of these is love.*

Jesus told His disciples, *By this all will know that you are My disciples, if you have love for one another* (John 13:32). Let's be known as disciples for Jesus.

# Chapter 5
## Doctrine of Man
# ANTHROPOLOGY

A. The Origin of Man

B. The Nature of Man

C. The Fall of Man

D. The Redemption of Man

# Doctrine of Man
# Anthropology
Greek words: *anthropos* means "man," and
*ology* comes from *logos* which means "account" or "reason"

*I have made the earth, And created man on it. I—
My hands—stretched out the heavens, And all their host I
have commanded* (Isaiah 45:12).

## A. The Origin of Man

A. W. Tozer summarized the creation of man perfectly when he
said, "God made us for Himself: that is the first and last thing
that can be said about human existence and whatever we add is
but commentary."

Man was made in the image or likeness of God. That is to say,
man was made to resemble God:

> *Then God said, "Let Us make man in Our image, according
> to Our likeness; let them have dominion over the fish of the
> sea, over the birds of the air, and over the cattle, over all the
> earth and over every creeping thing that creeps on the earth"*
> (Genesis 1:26).

God created man out of the dirt of the earth and breathed life
into him: *And the LORD God formed man of the dust of the ground,
and breathed into his nostrils the breath of life; and man became a living
being* (Genesis 2:7).

We know God made man an intelligent creation, because God
had him name all the animals in the Garden:

> *Out of the ground the LORD God formed every beast of the
> field and every bird of the air, and brought them to Adam to
> see what he would call them. And whatever Adam called each
> living creature, that was its name* (Genesis 2:19).

Because of the intelligence of man, we know we did not evolve from apes, as evolution would have us believe. As we read in Genesis 1:27, man was created in God's image and given dominion over every living thing. While the animals were created before man, they were not superior to man. The Bible specifically tells us, in Genesis 1:26, that the Triune God created man *in Our image, according to Our likeness.*

Man is the *crown* or *capstone* of creation (Genesis 1:26-28; Psalm 8:3-5). Even as sinners, we are still valuable to God, because we are made in His very image. None of us is an accident (Psalm 139:16) because we are all fearfully and wonderfully made (Psalm 139:14), and God does not make "junk."

Our value to God is so great that He sent Jesus to become a man and die for our sins (John 3:16; Philippians 2:6-8). If God loves sinners like us, we ought to love others (1 John 4:7-11) and have a passion for a lost and dying world (Matthew 9:36-38; Luke 15:1-24), especially for the youth, who are the future of the church and the world (Mark 10:13-15).

## B. The Nature of Man

Man was created with a triune nature—body, soul, and spirit:

> *Now may the God of peace Himself sanctify you completely; and may your whole spirit, soul, and body be preserved blameless at the coming of our Lord Jesus Christ* (1 Thessalonians 5:23).

The *body* is flesh, bones and blood — our physical being. The *soul* can be viewed as our mind, will and our emotions—our self-awareness. The *spirit* is that part in us which communes with God — our God-consciousness. The spirit sets us apart from all other creatures. It is our spirit that allows us to have intimate fellowship with God. When a man dies, his spirit departs from the body and either goes to be with the Lord or is lost enternally.

While the body is physical, the soul and spirit are non-physical and are tightly woven together (Hebrews 4:12). The soul of man submits to either his sinful nature or to the Spirit of God. The spirit of man enables him to enter into a personal relationship with God. When we are indwelt with the Spirit of God, our spirit becomes the very source of our worship, prayer and service to God: *The Spirit Himself bears witness with our spirit that we are children of God* (Romans 8:16).

American theologian, Cyrus Scofield clearly defines the role of the body, soul, and spirit:

> Because man is a *spirit*, he is capable of God-consciousness, and of communion with God; because he is *soul*, he has self-consciousness; because he is *body*, he has, through his senses, world-consciousness.

Man was created in God's image, endowing him with characteristics not found in any other creation of God. Animals exist and think in a purely instinctual way. Man was given moral character, allowing him to know right from wrong; reason, along with the ability to invent and create; and dominion over the earth and the animals in it:

> *Then God said, "Let Us make man in Our image, according to Our likeness; let them have dominion over the fish of the sea, over the birds of the air, and over the cattle, over all the earth and over every creeping thing that creeps on the earth"* (Genesis 1:26).

"Man's only claim to importance is that he was created in the divine image; in himself he is nothing."

—A.W. Tozer

## C. The Fall of Man

In Genesis 3, we read about the fall of man. This account does not introduce sin; it already existed. We see this in the rebellion of Satan. He fell in the sin of pride. In this section, we see how sin entered the human race (Isaiah 14:12-15). God created man *in His image*, without sin, but now we see how sin became part of mankind.

Man was made in God's image, so we know that man was created with intelligence, emotion and his own will. He was created without sin and put in a perfect environment, the Garden of Eden, but Adam and Eve chose to exercise their own will and rebel against God—to sin.

They knew they were not to eat of the tree of life, because God had instructed them in Genesis 2:16-17:

> *And the LORD God commanded the man, saying, "Of every tree of the garden you may freely eat; but of the tree of the knowledge of good and evil you shall not eat, for in the day that you eat of it you shall surely die."*

They willingly ate of the tree, against the command of God, resulting in the fallen nature of mankind. That nature has been passed on from generation to generation, as explained in Romans 5:12, *Therefore, just as through one man sin entered the world, and death through sin, and thus death spread to all men, because all sinned.*

## D. The Redemption of Man

You now know that God made man in His own image, without sin; but Adam and Eve chose to sin against God, bringing all of us under the condemnation of sin. However, it does not end there—we have hope.

Romans 5:18 tells us while one man, Adam, brought us under sin, one Man, Christ, paid the price to redeem us from our sin:

*Therefore, as through one man's offense judgment came to all
men, resulting in condemnation, even so through one Man's
righteous act the free gift came to all men, resulting in
justification of life.*

So, what is *redemption*, and how can one man redeem us? According
to *Vine's Expository Dictionary of Biblical Words*:

To *redeem* denotes "to buy out," especially of purchasing a
slave with a view to his freedom. It is used metaphorically
in Galatians 3:13 and 4:5, of the deliverance by Christ of
Christian Jews from the Law and its curse.

Redemption, *lutrosis* in the Greek, speaks of the redemptive work
of Christ, bringing deliverance through His death from the guilt
and power of sin.

The atoning work of Christ redeems us:

*Not with the blood of goats and calves, but with His own
blood He entered the Most Holy Place once for all, having
obtained eternal redemption* (Hebrews 9:12).

While the Jewish nation killed animals, using their blood as
a temporary covering, or atonement, for their sins, it is only
through the blood of Christ and His atoning work that we can be
covered once and for all for our sins:

*He has delivered us from the power of darkness and conveyed
us into the kingdom of the Son of His love, in whom we
have redemption through His blood, the forgiveness of sins*
(Colossians 1:13-14).

*In Him we have redemption through His blood, the forgiveness
of sins, according to the riches of His grace* (Ephesians 1:7).

Christ's redemption is for all of us, not just a few, because we all
are in need of His atoning blood. We are all born into sin and
have inherited the sinful nature of our parents, Adam and Eve,
but Christ has redeemed us and paid the price for our sins:

*For all have sinned and fall short of the glory of God, being justified freely by His grace through the redemption that is in Christ Jesus* (Romans 3:23-24).

*Who* [Christ] *gave Himself for us, that He might redeem us from every lawless deed and purify for Himself His own special people, zealous for good works* (Titus 2:14).

# Chapter 6

## DOCTRINE OF SIN
## HAMARTIOLOGY

A. The Fact of Sin

B. The Origin of Sin

C. The Nature of Sin

D. The Consequences of Sin

E. The Defeat of Sin

# Doctrine of Sin
# Hamartiology

Greek words: *hamartia* means "sin," and *ology*, "knowledge"

*"Woe to the rebellious children," says the LORD, "Who take counsel, but not of Me, And who devise plans, but not of My Spirit, That they may add sin to sin"* (Isaiah 30:1).

## A. The Fact of Sin

There are many who would argue that sin is a Christian concept and not a reality, but if we look at the history of man and the atrocities committed against one another, we simply cannot deny its existence.

Paul tells us in Romans 3:23, *for all have sinned and fall short of the glory of God.* If we have all sinned, then it must be part of man's character.

## B. The Origin of Sin

Sin did not begin on the earth in the Garden of Eden. It was first seen in heaven when Satan and many angels rebelled against God and He cast them out of heaven. Satan's sin was rebellion against God; he wanted to be exalted above God (Isaiah 14:12-15; Ezekiel 28:12-19): *"I [the Son of God] saw Satan fall like lighting from heaven"* (Luke 10:18).

In Genesis 3, we see how sin entered into our world. Adam and Eve lived in a perfect world. The Garden of Eden was beyond our imagination or expectations. Adam and Eve, themselves, were made in the image of God, so they were made without sin.

When the serpent came to Eve and tempted her with the forbidden fruit, she rebelled against God, ate the fruit and sin entered in. Then Eve brought the fruit to Adam, and he, too, rebelled against God and ate the fruit, joining her in the sin.

After the temptation and the fall into sin, we see the emergence of guilt. Adam and Eve both knew they had done wrong, so they hid from God:

> *And they heard the sound of the LORD God walking in the garden in the cool of the day, and Adam and his wife hid themselves from the presence of the LORD God among the trees of the garden* (Genesis 3:8).

We all try to hide from God, from our family and from our friends when we do things we know are wrong. We try to hide our sins in the darkness, thinking no one will find out. Remember, we can hide from the world, but God knows our hearts and sees our sins, even in the dark:

> *And there is no creature hidden from His sight, but all things are naked and open to the eyes of Him to whom we must give account* (Hebrews 4:13).

## C.  The Nature of Sin

In the Hebrew and Greek languages, there are many words used for sin, depending upon the type of sin. In the area of morals, one of the most common Greek words used for *sin* in Romans 3:23 and 5:12, is defined "to miss the mark." Another word used literally means "crookedness" and is often translated as "perverseness." It also pertains to our breaking God's Law or lawlessness (1 John 3:4).

In relationship to our conduct with one another, the word used for *sin* means "violence or conduct which causes injury" (Ezekiel 7:23).

*Sin* in regard to truth is translated as "speaking falsely" or "deceitfully"—bearing false witness. The first sinner was a liar, Satan (John 8:44), and the first sin on earth began with a lie when he lied to Eve in the Garden of Eden (Genesis 3:4).

Other words used for sin include: *iniquity* (Leviticus 26:40); *godlessness* (1 Peter 4:8); *wickedness* (Proverbs 11:31); *unbelief* (Romans 11:20); *unrighteousness* (1 John 1:9); *unholiness* (1 Timothy 1:9) and *unjustness* (Deuteronomy 25:16).

## D. The Consequences of Sin

*For the wages of sin is death, but the gift of God is eternal life in Christ Jesus our Lord* (Romans 6:23).

Ultimately, the consequence of sin is death. It may be spiritual death while we are alive and become separated from God, because we are in a sinful state; or it is eternal death when we die physically in that sinful state and enter eternity separated from God.

When we sin, we not only experience death, but we experience the law of sowing and reaping. While God will forgive us of our sins, there are often consequences to the sins we commit. Those consequences must be faced, regardless of the gift of forgiveness God gives us: *Even as I have seen, Those who plow iniquity And sow trouble reap the same* (Job 4:8).

For example, if we lie all the time and then ask God for forgiveness, He will forgive us, but we are left with a reputation as a liar. We are reaping the consequences of the lies we have sown!

## E. The Defeat of Sin

Let's go back to that verse in Romans: *For the wages of sin is death, but the gift of God is eternal life in Christ Jesus our Lord* (Romans 6:23).

This verse does not end with *death*, but *eternal life in Christ Jesus.* While the consequence of sin is death, God offers us the gift of eternal life, because sin was defeated by Christ on the cross with His atoning blood.

I once saw a black and white print that showed an old, rugged cross with a scroll unfurled and nailed to it, covered with blood.

It was awesome because I knew that scroll represented all my sins, nailed to the cross that once held Jesus. It is now unable to be read, because the blood of Jesus Christ covered it.

> *He . . . having forgiven you all trespasses, having wiped out the handwriting of requirements that was against us, which was contrary to us. And He has taken it out of the way, having nailed it to the cross* (Colossians 2:13-14).

Because He was sinless, Christ was the only One who could pay the penalty for our sin and redeem us with His sacrifice: *For He made Him who knew no sin to be sin for us, that we might become the righteousness of God in Him* (2 Corinthians 5:21).

We can choose to live in our sins, condemned, or live a life of victory, with Christ. He died upon the cross, defeating sin and death. Let's choose life in Christ, not death in sin.

# Chapter 7

# DOCTRINE OF SALVATION

# SOTERIOLOGY

A. The Nature of Salvation

B. Repentance and Faith

C. Regeneration

D. Justification

E. Redemption

F. Sanctification

G. Glorification

H. Abiding in Christ – Obedience

# DOCTRINE OF SALVATION
# SOTERIOLOGY

Greek words: *soteria* means "salvation," and
*ology* comes from *logos* which means "discourse" or "reason"

*"Behold, God is my salvation, I will trust and not be afraid;
'For YAH, the LORD, is my strength and song; He also has
become my salvation' "* (Isaiah 12:2).

## A. The Nature of Salvation

Christ purchased our salvation through His atoning death upon
the cross, and when we accept Him as our personal Savior, we
receive His redeeming grace. There are two parts to salvation:
how God applies it to our lives and how we receive it into our
lives. While we do nothing to earn salvation because it is a gift
of God, purchased with the blood of Jesus Christ, we must *accept*
the gift that God freely offers us.

What does God offer us? He offers us *regeneration, justification,
redemption, sanctification* and *glorification*, if we will only *repent*, have
*faith* and *abide* in Him by being obedient to Him.

When we repent and accept Jesus Christ as our personal Lord
and Savior, we establish a personal relationship with Him. Before
confessing Him by faith, we are enemies of God (Romans 5:10)
because our sins have separated us from Him. The Bible says, *But
your iniquities* [sins] *have separated you from your God* (Isaiah 59:2).

Salvation sets us free from the bondage of sin and puts us under
the Lordship of Jesus Christ. Before accepting Jesus, we were
ruled by sin, but now we are ruled by the Spirit.

Romans 8:5 says, *For those who live according to the flesh set their
minds on the things of the flesh, but those who live according to the Spirit,
the things of the Spirit.*

God not only saves us spiritually, but physically, emotionally, relationally and in every other way. He is a great God and Savior, and wants to be our All in All. The Bible tells us that those who call on the Lord will be saved (Romans 10:13).

## B. Repentance and Faith

*Repentance* is a turning away from sin—a change of mind, heart and actions. It is realizing, intellectually, that your actions are not right, followed by remorse or sadness concerning the actions, resulting in a change in attitude and actions. When we repent, we make a 180 degree turn from our original heading, leading us in the opposite direction, toward Christ.

To put it simply, we must realize we are sinners, confess our sins to God and turn away from sin.

Repentance was the message preached by John the Baptist in Matthew 3:1-2: *In those days John the Baptist came preaching in the wilderness of Judea, and saying, "Repent, for the kingdom of heaven is at hand!"*

In Mark 2:17, we see that this was also Jesus' message: *When Jesus heard it, He said to them, "Those who are well have no need of a physician, but those who are sick. I did not come to call the righteous, but sinners, to repentance."*

Later, Jesus called His Apostles to deliver this same message in Luke 24:46, 47

> *Then He said to them, "Thus it is written, and thus it was necessary for the Christ to suffer and to rise from the dead the third day, and that repentance and remission of sins should be preached in His name to all nations, beginning at Jerusalem."*

We must keep in mind that God cannot be fooled—He knows our hearts, so we cannot fake repentance. Without true and genuine repentance, a sinner cannot be saved (Hebrews 12:15-17).

Like repentance, *faith* requires action intellectually, emotionally and willfully. It is a commitment to the knowledge of the truth of God's Word, followed by an emotional attachment to follow the truths of the Bible, while submitting our will to the will of God. In other words, you recognize that the Bible is the true Word of God. You read it and see a change in your life, as you submit your will to the Lord, seeking Him in all that you do: *For we walk by faith, not by sight* (2 Corinthians 5:7).

In Hebrews 11:1, we see the best definition of faith: *Now faith is the substance of things hoped for, the evidence of things not seen.* The word *substance* is in reference to faith being the foundation of our hope in Christ Jesus.

Our hope is in Christ and not in ourselves, because we cannot earn our way into heaven. Ephesians 2:8-9 tells us we are saved through faith: *For by grace you have been saved through faith, and that not of yourselves; it is the gift of God, not of works, lest anyone should boast.*

But it is not just faith in something or anything; it is faith in Jesus Christ that saves us. This is saving faith:

> *But these* [signs that Jesus did] *are written that you may believe that Jesus is the Christ, the Son of God, and that believing you may have life in His name* (John 20:31).

> *But what does it* [the Scriptures] *say? "The word is near you, in your mouth and in your heart" (that is, the word of faith which we preach): that if you confess with your mouth the Lord Jesus and believe in your heart that God has raised Him from the dead, you will be saved. For with the heart one believes unto righteousness, and with the mouth confession is made unto salvation* (Romans 10:8-10).

> *For this reason I also suffer these things; nevertheless I am not ashamed, for I know whom I have believed and am persuaded that He is able to keep what I have committed to Him until that Day* (2 Timothy 1:12).

> *For "whoever calls on the name of the LORD shall be saved."*
> *How then shall they call on Him in whom they have not believed?*
> (Romans 10:13-14).

> *Now the just shall live by faith; But if anyone draws back,*
> *My soul has no pleasure in him. But we are not of those who*
> *draw back to perdition, but of those who believe to the saving*
> *of the soul* (Hebrews 10:38-39).

In Ephesians 2:9, it says we are saved by faith, not works, so you may wonder how works fit into the picture of salvation. James, the brother of Jesus, explains it perfectly in his Book—just read James 2:14-26. The key verse is James 2:18, *But someone will say, "You have faith, and I have works." Show me your faith without your works, and I will show you my faith by my works.* You see, works come out of, or are a product of, our faith; the works do not produce faith or salvation.

In order to make a complete commitment to the truths of the Bible, our faith cannot be a "blind faith." It must be faith, based upon knowledge—knowledge of His Word and of His Person. In Romans 10:17, we see this truth: *So then faith comes by hearing, and hearing by the word of God.*

So, in order to walk by faith, we must know the Word of God, through which we will come to have a personal relationship with God the Father, His Son, and the Holy Spirit.

Simply put, faith is believing the promises of God and taking Him at His Word.

## C. Regeneration

In *Webster's*, *regeneration* is defined as: "The act of being spiritually reborn; complete reformation; bringing into existence again; the act of being made anew or formed again."

In the New Testament, the new birth is described as a cleansing: *According to His mercy He saved us, through the washing of regeneration* (Titus 3:5). It is also described as being *born again* (John 3:3, 5-6).

Man was created with three aspects to his nature: a *body*, a *soul*, and a *spirit*. God designed us to have our spirit (nature of man that communes with God) rule over our body (physical being) and soul (our intellect, will and our emotional being). Because of our rebellion against God, things were turned around, and we became spiritually dead, allowing our body and soul to rule our spirit.

God wants to indwell us with His Spirit through regeneration, reviving our spirit, so we no longer walk according to the flesh, but in the Spirit. Then, walking in the Spirit, we will experience a new life; born again of the Spirit, we can now understand the things of God.

In Romans 6:4, Paul referred to this new birth as *newness of life*. Peter described it as being *begotten again* (1 Peter 1:3). Therefore, if you have not been born again, you cannot enter the kingdom of God:

> *Jesus answered and said to him, "Most assuredly, I say to you, unless one is born again, he cannot see the kingdom of God"* (John 3:3).

> *Not by works of righteousness which we have done, but according to His mercy He saved us, through the washing of regeneration and renewing of the Holy Spirit* (Titus 3:5).

While we are made new through regeneration, we are placed into the family of God through adoption. According to *Webster's*, *adopt* means "to take into a new relationship." Paul tells us that we are adopted as sons (and daughters), through Christ:

> *God sent His Son . . . to redeem those who were under the law, that we might receive the adoption as sons* (Galatians 4:5).

> *God . . . having predestined us to adoption as sons by Jesus Christ to Himself, according to the good pleasure of His will* (Ephesians 1:5).

# D. Justification

*Justification* is God's provision of salvation for guilty and lost sinners. Because of Christ's redeeming work—His death on the cross—we no longer stand before God as sinners, unrighteous or guilty, but as holy, righteous and not guilty. We are declared righteous because of our faith in Christ (Romans 4:5).

We are declared righteous the moment we accept Jesus Christ as our Lord and Savior. We are not only born again, our old self dies and a new spiritual man arises. This new man is freed from the stain of sin in the eyes of God. This does not mean that he will not sin again; he has not become sinless. It means that he is forgiven and seen as sinless in the eyes of God.

The term *justification* means that the believer is in "right standing before God." It speaks of a courtroom scene in which the accused is acquitted and pronounced "not guilty." To help us remember what it means to be justified, it is sometimes broken up in the following manner: "just-if-ied" never sinned or "just as if I'd never sinned:"

> *For all have sinned and fall short of the glory of God, being justified freely by His grace through the redemption that is in Christ Jesus, whom God set forth as a propitiation by His blood, through faith, to demonstrate His righteousness, because in His forbearance God had passed over the sins that were previously committed, to demonstrate at the present time His righteousness, that He might be just and the justifier of the one who has faith in Jesus* (Romans 3:23-26).

While regeneration and justification are closely related doctrines, Thiessen's summary clearly defines the difference: "In regeneration we receive a new life; in justification, a new standing; and in adoption, a new position."

## E. Redemption

The word *redeemed* in both the Old and New Testaments speaks of "buying something back at a price" or "to free from bondage by paying a price." In the Old Testament, in the Book of Ruth, we see a foreshadow of our Redeemer in Boaz, Ruth's kinsman redeemer, *goel* in Hebrew.

In Israel, the *goel* was the nearest living male, blood relative. He had certain responsibilities toward his next of kin. If a family member was too poor to redeem their inheritance, it was the duty of the kinsman to redeem it (Leviticus 25:25, 28; Ruth 3:9, 12). The kinsman was also required to redeem any relative who had sold themselves into slavery.

Ruth was a foreigner, not a Jew, who came to Israel with her mother-in-law, Naomi, after all the men in their family had died. Naomi returned to Israel with nothing, only her daughter-in-law, Ruth.

However, the Lord provided a kinsman redeemer for them. He brought Ruth to the farm of Boaz, and although Boaz was not the next in line to redeem the land of Naomi's husband, he challenged the relative next in line and purchased, not only the land, but the right to marry Ruth. Boaz redeemed the land for Naomi, bringing the land of her husband back to the family and freeing Naomi and Ruth from a life of poverty.

In the New Testament, we see the true Redeemer, Jesus Christ, who died on the cross and paid the ultimate price for our freedom from sin. Jesus is the *Goel* of His people (Exodus 6:6; Job 19:25; Psalm 103:4; Isaiah 41:14, 43:1, 44:6, 22, 48:20).

*In Him we have redemption through His blood, the forgiveness of sins, according to the riches of His grace which He made to abound toward us in all wisdom and prudence* (Ephesians 1:7-8).

The word *redemption* has a double significance; it means "the payment of a price," as well as "the deliverance of the captive." According to the Word of God, the death of Christ on the cross is the price Jesus paid for the deliverance of the sinner, and He said, *"The Son of Man did not come to be served, but to serve, and to give His life a ransom for many"* (Matthew 20:28).

Not to be taken lightly, Paul reminded the Corinthians of the great price that was paid for our salvation in 1 Corinthians 6:19-20: *For you were bought at a price; therefore glorify God in your body and in your spirit, which are God's.*

We must always remember that the deliverance which Jesus bought for us through His work on the cross could not be obtained through any other means or any other man, and it was bought at a tremendous price: *Not with the blood of goats and calves, but with His own blood He entered the Most Holy Place once for all, having obtained eternal redemption* (Hebrews 9:12).

## F. Sanctification

The term *sanctification* means "to be made holy" and "to be set apart." Sanctification speaks of both a position and a process in the Christian life. The moment we are born again, positionally, we are sanctified, made holy, and set apart for God's purpose. Every Christian needs to understand that they have been sanctified and set apart for a special purpose for the glory of God.

Sanctification includes both a "separation from" and a "dedication to." We are to separate ourselves from the world and commit ourselves to God. They are not exclusive to each other.

Being set apart for God involves relationship and service. Just as a man sets himself apart for his wife and no other woman—he shares a unique relationship with her—so, we are to be set apart in our relationship to God. In regard to service, God called those instruments and utensils to be used in the Tabernacle service, holy. Why? Because they were to be used exclusively for His service alone, and not for common use. These two concepts of separation and service apply to us and our lives.

This is seen in the life of Jeremiah: *Before I formed you in the womb I knew you; Before you were born I sanctified you; I ordained you a prophet to the nations* (Jeremiah 1:5). Jeremiah, though born into sin, was called to walk holy before God and be set apart for the service of God.

As we behold the LORD through His Word and intimate communion with Him, we are being changed into His likeness (2 Corinthians 3:18). We do not become sinless, but we do sin less. As we walk with Him, we live more holy lives. The Bible says in Galatians 5:16, *I say then; walk in the Spirit, and you shall not fulfill the lust of the flesh.* So, this process begins the moment we are justified and continues up until the moment when we die.

## G. Glorification

*Glorification* refers to the final, eternal state of the believer. It speaks of the believer acquiring a new, heavenly or glorified body at the moment of death (Romans 8:30b; Philippians 3:21). The Bible says that when believers die, *we shall not be found naked . . . but further clothed, that mortality may be swallowed up by life* (2 Corinthians 5:3-4). Paul also states in 2 Corinthians 5:8 that *to be absent from the body* [is] *to be present with the Lord.*

For the believer, death is a glorious thing. In heaven there is no sickness, temptation, sorrow or death:

> *And God will wipe away every tear from their eyes; there shall be no more death, nor sorrow, nor crying. There shall be no more pain, for the former things have passed away* (Revelation 21:4).

Also, the saints from all the ages, since the beginning of time, are reunited with their Creator, who loved us before the foundation of the world (John 17:24).

## H. Abiding in Christ – Obedience

The primary reference for *abiding* is in John 15:1-8, which describes the relationship that exists between God and believers. Those who neglect to abide in Him are cast out and in danger of judgment (Matthew 7:21-23). Those who do abide in Christ are not only considered true disciples, but their lives will produce much fruit (Galatians 5:22-23).

The Christian must both believe and abide in Christ. The word *believe* in the following passages, and others such as John 3:16 and John 6:40, is in the present tense, and it means "to believe and to continue to believe" or "to abide." It implies not only an initial act of faith, but a maintained attitude of faith.

Even though God does not desire that anyone should perish for all eternity, God does not save or keep a man against his will (Hebrews 2:3). As Jude 21 says, *keep yourselves in the love of God, looking for the mercy of our Lord Jesus Christ unto eternal life.* Just as faith in God and repentance from sin are necessary for salvation, so they are necessary for the continuance of the Christian's life. The scriptural condition for salvation is believing:

> He who believes in the Son has everlasting life; and he who does not believe the Son shall not see life, but the wrath of God abides on him (John 3:36).

> He who believes in Him is not condemned; but he who does not believe is condemned already, because he has not believed in the name of the Only Begotten Son of God (John 3:18).

Remember, throughout the Old Testament, it has always been God's heart that all should come to repentance, and no one would be lost (2 Peter 3:9), but it is our choice. God tells us in Isaiah 43:11, *"I, even I, am the LORD, and besides Me there is no other savior."*

# Chapter 3
# DOCTRINE OF THE CHURCH
# ECCLESIOLOGY

## A. The Nature of the Church

Titles of the New Testament Church
1. Brethren
2. Believers
3. Saints
4. The Elect
5. Disciples
6. Christians
7. Those of the Way

Illustrations of the Church
1. The Body of Christ
2. The Temple of God
3. The Bride of Christ

## B. The Founding of the Church

## C. The Work of the Church
1. Proclaim the Good News
2. Be Salt and Light
3. Worship and Glorify God
4. Fellowship

## D. The Worship of the Church

## E. The Organization of the Church

# DOCTRINE OF THE CHURCH
# ECCLESIOLOGY
Greek word: *ekklesia* means "an assembly of people"

*And I also say to you that you are Peter, and on this rock I will build My church, and the gates of Hades shall not prevail against it* (Matthew 16:18).

## A. The Nature of the Church

The very nature of the Church is revealed in the Greek words used in the New Testament. The *church* is referred to as the *Ekklesia*, which is Greek for "an assembly of called out ones." The English word *church* comes from the Greek word *kurikon* meaning "that which belongs to the Lord."

From these two words alone, we can conclude that the Church consists of those called out of the world who belong to the Lord.

There are also a number of titles or terms used in the New Testament when referring to the Church. Here are a few:

1.  **Brethren**: *Brethren, let each one remain with God in that state in which he was called* (1 Corinthians 7:24).

The term *brethren* literally means brother from the same parents or parent. In the Christian faith, the term brethren is applied to "one of the same faith." As Christians, we are all brothers and sisters because we have the same Father (Ephesians 3:14-15).

2.  **Believers**: *And believers were increasingly added to the Lord, multitudes of both men and women* (Acts 5:14).

The title of *believer* speaks of one connected by the common denominator of the Christian faith.

**3. Saints:** *To the saints and faithful brethren in Christ who are in Colosse* (Colossians 1:2).

The term *saints* means "set apart ones." By this definition, all who are believers in Christ are saints. It is not designated for only those who are more holy, because we all fall short.

**4. The Elect:** *Who shall bring a charge against God's elect? It is God who justifies* (Romans 8:33). *Therefore, as the elect of God, holy and beloved, put on tender mercies, kindness, humility, meekness, longsuffering* (Colossians 3:12).

The *elect* are Jew and Gentile believers who have been chosen or picked out (Ephesians 1:4).

**5. Disciples:** *Then Jesus said to those Jews who believed Him, "If you abide in My word, you are My disciples indeed"* (John 8:31).

The word *disciple* literally means "learner." It designates a person who follows another person's teaching. So, the Apostles were disciples of Christ as they followed His teachings, and today, we are all disciples of Christ if we follow the Bible, which contains His teaching.

**6. Christians:** *And the disciples were first called Christians in Antioch* (Acts 11:26).

The early believers did not originally adopt this title. *Christian* was given to them by others, and it meant that they were "followers of Jesus Christ." It was not until the second century that believers accepted this as a title of honor.

**7. Those of the Way:** *Saul . . . asked letters from him* [high priest] *to the synagogues of Damascus, so that if he found any who were of the Way, whether men or women, he might bring them bound to Jerusalem* (Acts 9:1-2).

The early Christians were called this because they followed the *way* or *course* prescribed by Christ. Jesus called Himself

The Way (Matthew 7:13-14; John 14:6) and opened a new and living way to God (Hebrews 10:19-20).

Regardless of the title or term used, all of them point back to Jesus Christ and the fact that we are all followers or learners of Christ. We have been chosen by God our Father to believe in Him and His Son, to walk in such a way that people see Christ in us.

Finally, the nature of the Church is revealed in three illustrations of the Church: the *Body of Christ*, the *Temple of God* and the *Bride of Christ*.

1.  **The Body of Christ**: *Now you are the body of Christ, and members individually* (1 Corinthians 12:27).

Christ is the Head of the Church and the Church is the Body of Christ. He has called us to continue His work on this earth. Of course, we are not sinless, and we may not perform miracles, but as Christ preached the Good News of the coming Kingdom, so we must also do.

2.  **The Temple of God**: *And what agreement has the temple of God with idols? For you are the temple of the living God. As God has said: "I will dwell in them And walk among them. I will be their God, And they shall be My people"* (2 Corinthians 6:16).

In the Old Testament, God met with His people in the Temple. Now, in the New Testament, God is with us and dwells in us. We do not have to go to the Temple to meet with God; we are His temple where He dwells. God no longer limits His dwelling presence to a stationary building, but goes out to every man and woman through each believer who He indwells (2 Corinthians 5:20).

3.  **The Bride of Christ**: *Then I, John, saw the holy city, New Jerusalem, coming down out of heaven from God, prepared as a bride adorned for her husband* (Revelation 21:2).

The Church is the Bride of Christ. As the bridegroom has intimate relationship with his bride and is the head of his wife and family, Christ is the head of the Church, loving and caring for us—giving His very life for us. As the Church, we submit to Christ, our Head. The beauty and radiance of the Bride is seen only in our submission and obedience to Him (Ephesians 5:22-33).

## B. The Founding of the Church

The forming of the Church was foretold by Jesus in Matthew 16:18 when He said, *"And I also say to you that you are Peter, and on this rock I will build My church, and the gates of Hades shall not prevail against it."*

Jesus was not saying the Church would be built upon Peter, but upon his profession that Christ was the Son of God: *Simon Peter answered and said, "You are the Christ, the Son of the living God"* (Matthew 16:16).

The promise of the Church in Matthew 16:18 was fulfilled in Acts 1-2, and by the end of these two chapters, we see the Church already growing: *And the Lord added to the church daily those who were being saved* (Acts 2:47).

As the Lord was adding to the Church, He was also sending the Apostles out on the commission to tell the world about the saving grace of Jesus Christ, saying, *"But you shall receive power when the Holy Spirit has come upon you; and you shall be witnesses to Me in Jerusalem, and in all Judea and Samaria, and to the end of the earth"* (Acts 1:8).

Throughout the New Testament writings, we see churches formed as the good news was shared by the Apostles and disciples. As people came to the Lord, the people would gather in the temple (Acts 5:12), and in homes (Acts 2:46, 12:12), for prayer (Acts 3:1, 10:9), and for communion (Acts 2:42, 46, 20:7).

## C. The Work of the Church

There are four main purposes for the Church in this world. They are designed to either reveal God to the world or to edify the members of the congregation.

### 1. Proclaim the Good News

First and foremost, we are to *proclaim* the Good News of Jesus Christ and the salvation He provides for us, as He instructed in Matthew 28:19-20:

> *"Go therefore and make disciples of all the nations, baptizing them in the name of the Father and of the Son and of the Holy Spirit, teaching them to observe all things that I have commanded you; and lo, I am with you always, even to the end of the age." Amen*

> *And He said to them, "Go into all the world and preach the gospel to every creature"* (Mark 16:15).

### 2. Be Salt and Light

Second, we are to be *salt and light* to the world, providing the moral standard demonstrated to us by Christ:

> *You are the salt of the earth; but if the salt loses its flavor, how shall it be seasoned? It is then good for nothing but to be thrown out and trampled underfoot by men* (Matthew 5:13).

> *Let your light so shine before men, that they may see your good works and glorify your Father in heaven (Matthew 5:16).*

> *For it is the God who commanded light to shine out of darkness, who has shone in our hearts to give the light of the knowledge of the glory of God in the face of Jesus Christ* (2 Corinthians 4:6).

Are you being salt and light among your school mates, your co-workers or your family? Do the people around you know that you are followers of Christ, or do you hide the light of Jesus Christ under a table? Are your conversations lacking the salt and seasoning of Jesus Christ? When I got saved, the light of Jesus Christ beamed from me, and my conversation was all about Jesus Christ. No one was left in doubt that I was a Christian. Still, today, I continually share the Word of God with the people I encounter. Remember, we have nothing to offer this world if we are not giving them Jesus Christ. Be salt and light to a dark and tasteless world.

### 3. Worship and Glorify God

Third, as the angels in heaven *worship and glorify* God, we are to worship and glorify Him here on earth: *Therefore by Him let us continually offer the sacrifice of praise to God, that is, the fruit of our lips, giving thanks to His name* (Hebrews 13:15).

As you know, we worship the Lord when we sing praise and worship songs to Him. But, did you know, we worship and glorify the Lord when we walk according to His Word? We worship Him in our tithes, and we worship and glorify Him when we sit in church, learn the Bible and apply His teachings to our lives. God is glorified by our obedience to Him.

### 4. Fellowship

Fourth, the church provides *fellowship* for believers to build up, encourage and admonish one another:

> Bear one another's burdens, and so fulfill the law of Christ (Galatians 6:2).

> But if we walk in the light as He is in the light, we have fellowship with one another, and the blood of Jesus Christ His Son cleanses us from all sin (1 John 1:7).

> And let us consider one another in order to stir up love and good works, not forsaking the assembling of ourselves

*together, as is the manner of some, but exhorting one another, and so much the more as you see the Day approaching* (Hebrews 10:24-25).

*As iron sharpens iron, So a man sharpens the countenance of his friend* (Proverbs 27:17).

In order to be spiritually strong, the Bible tells us we must do three things: pray, read God's Word and be in fellowship. Many do the first two, but do not think fellowship is important in their walk with the Lord. If it was not important, God would not have told us to have fellowship, one with another. As believers, we are in fellowship for a number of reasons, but one of the most important is accountability, which is the key in Proverbs 27:17. We sharpen each other as we hold each other accountable in our walks with the Lord. We also build up one another as we go through trials. I cannot stress more the importance of fellowship, because I have seen many walk away from the Lord as their fellowship in the church diminished.

## D. The Worship of the Church

Worship is at the center of our Christian experience. It is the way in which we please and glorify God. But the only way to truly and rightfully worship God is to understand and appreciate His love for us.

*Worship* is the natural response to God, because it is the outgrowth of a personal relationship with Him. If we do not understand who He is, what He has done and what He desires for us, it will be impossible for us to enter into true worship.

We must also understand that we do not worship because of what we can get, but because of who He is: *Behold, God is my salvation; I will trust, and not be afraid: for the Lord Jehovah is my Strength and my Song; He also is become my salvation* (Isaiah 12:2).

Worship involves our whole being: our emotional, intellectual, physical and spiritual self (Psalm 103:1). This is why Jesus said that God was looking for those who would worship Him in spirit and in truth:

> *But the hour is coming, and now is, when the true worshipers will worship the Father in spirit and truth; for the Father is seeking such to worship Him. God is Spirit, and those who worship Him must worship in spirit and truth* (John 4:23-24).

## E.  The Organization of the Church

The early church was comprised of Jews who influenced the organization and structure of the church. Since they already had a system in place for assembling and worshipping, the new church, or the Christian church, was patterned after the synagogue in some ways, which included meeting together to hear the Scriptures and meeting for prayer. However, Christ ordained *two rites*, also known as "sacraments," not practiced in the synagogues: *baptism* in Acts 2:38, *Then Peter said to them, "Repent, and let every one of you be baptized in the name of Jesus Christ for the remission of sins; and you shall receive the gift of the Holy Spirit,"* and *communion* in 1 Corinthians 10:16, *The cup of blessing which we bless, is it not the communion of the blood of Christ? The bread which we break, is it not the communion of the body of Christ?* (See also 1 Corinthians 11:23-26.)

We can see by the accounts in the Book of Acts that *offices* or *positions* in the church were filled as the needs arose. To begin with, the Apostles had the responsibility to study the Scriptures and proclaim the Gospel of Jesus Christ. Jesus gave them this commission Himself in Acts 1:8: *"But you shall receive power when the Holy Spirit has come upon you; and you shall be witnesses to Me in Jerusalem, and in all Judea and Samaria, and to the end of the earth."*

As they went out preaching about Jesus and establishing churches throughout Israel and the neighboring countries, they had the responsibility of maintaining the unity of the church. In each city, teachers, leaders and elders were set up in the churches to continue the work of building God's kingdom and feeding the flock (Acts 14:23; Titus 1:5). However, the Apostles had to oversee the various churches in order to maintain the integrity of the teachings of Christ.

As the congregation grew and more were added to the church, other leadership positions were needed to maintain unity and practice. We see in Acts 6:1-7 the first appointments of the church, and the qualifications to be in church leadership are found in verse 3: *Therefore, brethren, seek out from among you seven men of good reputation, full of the Holy Spirit and wisdom, whom we may appoint over this business.*

Throughout the Book of Acts and the Epistles, we see the organization of the church expand, beginning with the appointment of Stephen and the others to serve the congregation in Acts 6:2-6. Next, we see the election of elders, bishops, deacons and the presbytery in Acts 20:17; Philippians 1:1 and 1 Timothy 4:14. Last, we see the unity of the church through the letters Paul wrote to the churches (Ephesians 4:3). These letters were sent to encourage, admonish and keep in alignment the many churches scattered throughout Israel and the neighboring countries.

## Chapter 9
## DOCTRINE OF ANGELS
# ANGELOLOGY

## A. The Origin of Angels

## B. The Nature of Angels

Characteristics
1. Spirits
2. Human Bodies
3. Not to Be Worshipped
4. Immortal
5. Innumerable
6. Neither Male nor Female

## C. The Classification of Angels
1. Angel of the Lord
2. The Archangel
3. Angels of the Nations
4. Cherubim
5. Seraphim

## D. The Character and Attributes of Angels
1. Obedient
2. Reverent
3. Wise
4. Meek
5. Mighty
6. Holy

E.  The Ministry of Angels in Heaven

F.  The Ministry of Angels on Earth
God's Agents

God's Messengers
1. Announcements
2. Warnings
3. Instruction
4. Encouragement

God's Ministering Servants
1. They Sustain
2. They Preserve
3. They Deliver
4. They Intercede
5. They Minister to us after We Die
6. They Rejoice at our Salvation

G.  The Ranking and Function of Angels
1. Thrones
2. Dominions
3. Principalities and Authorities
4. Might
5. Powers

# DOCTRINE OF ANGELS
# ANGELOLOGY

Hebrew O.T. word *mal'ak*, and Greek N.T. word *aggelos* mean "messenger"

*Bless the LORD, you His angels, Who excel in strength, who do His word, Heeding the voice of His word. Bless the LORD, all you His hosts, You ministers of His, who do His pleasure* (Psalm 103:20-21).

While we live and exist in a physical world, there is a spiritual realm all around us in which the angels of God exist. We cannot see them, but they are all around us. Throughout the Bible, the writers have opened up windows into this spiritual realm, giving us a limited glance into it. Through these glimpses into the spiritual world, we see the nature and character of angels, teaching us through their example to be obedient to God.

## A. The Origin of Angels

*For by Him all things were created that are in heaven and that are on earth, visible and invisible, whether thrones or dominions or principalities or powers. All things were created through Him and for Him* (Colossians 1:16).

From this verse, we can conclude that angels are created beings. They were created by God, long before man. While the Scriptures do not give an exact time of creation, it is believed that they were created on the first day of Creation when God made the heavens and the earth.

In Job 38:4, 7, The Lord answered Job out of the whirlwind and said: *"Where were you when I laid the foundations of the earth? . . . And all the sons of God* [angels] *shouted for joy?"* From this we can conclude that the angels were there when He created the earth.

# B. The Nature of Angels

The nature of angels is revealed in the Scriptures, both in the Old and New Testaments, from the writings of the Old Testament prophets to the epistles of Paul the Apostle, to the final revelation given to John the Apostle. Throughout the ages, men have encountered angels and written of them.

## 1. Spirits

Angels are spirits, not having corporeal bodies, with the ability to move without limitations. They are in heaven with God and can also come to earth to minister to man:

> *Are they not all ministering spirits sent forth to minister for those who will inherit salvation?* (Hebrews 1:14).

> *Who makes His angels spirits, His ministers a flame of fire* (Psalms 104:4).

## 2. Human Bodies

They can assume the form of human bodies. Most often, we are not aware of angels because they exist in a heavenly realm, invisible to the human eye; but when needed, they can appear in human form for man to see:

> *Do not forget to entertain strangers, for by so doing some have unwittingly entertained angels* (Hebrews 13:2).

> *Now the two angels came to Sodom in the evening, and Lot was sitting in the gate of Sodom. When Lot saw them, he rose to meet them, and he bowed himself with his face toward the ground* (Genesis 19:1).

> *And she saw two angels in white sitting, one at the head and the other at the feet, where the body of Jesus had lain* (John 20:12).

> *Now an angel of the Lord spoke to Philip, saying, "Arise and go toward the south along the road which goes down from Jerusalem to Gaza." This is desert* (Acts 8:26).

### 3.  Not to be Worshipped

They are not to be worshipped. Many times throughout the Scriptures, men have tried to worship angels when they have appeared to them. In every instance, the angels have corrected the men and told them to worship only Jehovah, God.

> *Let no one cheat you of your reward, taking delight in false humility and worship of angels, intruding into those things which he has not seen, vainly puffed up by his fleshly mind* (Colossians 2:18).

> *Now I, John, saw and heard these things. And when I heard and saw, I fell down to worship before the feet of the angel who showed me these things. Then he said to me, "See that you do not do that. For I am your fellow servant, and of your brethren the prophets, and of those who keep the words of this book. Worship God"* (Revelation 22:8-9).

### 4.  Immortal

They are immortal. They cannot die, *"nor can they* [resurrected believers] *die anymore, for they are equal to the angels and are sons of God, being sons of the resurrection"* (Luke 20:36).

### 5.  Innumerable

They are vast in numbers. According to the Scriptures, their number is beyond human comprehension and calculations. Each one is as different and unique as each person on earth.

> *Is there any number to His armies? Upon whom does His light not rise?* (Job 25:3).

> *But you have come to Mount Zion and to the city of the living God, the heavenly Jerusalem, to an innumerable company of angels* (Hebrews 12:22).

> *Or do you think that I cannot now pray to My Father, and He will provide Me with more than twelve legions of angels?* (Matthew 26:53).

> *Then I looked, and I heard the voice of many angels around the throne, the living creatures, and the elders; and the number of them was ten thousand times ten thousand, and thousands of thousands* (Revelation 5:11).

### 6.  Neither Male nor Female

They are without sex, neither male nor female—not given in marriage nor reproducing themselves. The number of angels neither increases nor decreases because they do not die or reproduce.

> *For when they rise from the dead, they neither marry nor are given in marriage, but are like angels in heaven* (Mark 12:25).

> *But those who are counted worthy to attain that age, and the resurrection from the dead, neither marry nor are given in marriage; nor can they die anymore, for they are equal to the angels and are sons of God, being sons of the resurrection* (Luke 20:35-36).

## C.  The Classification of Angels

God is a God of order not confusion. The angels are referred to as an army in Joshua 5:15: *Then the Commander of the LORD's army said to Joshua, "Take your sandal off your foot, for the place where you stand is holy." And Joshua did so.* Therefore, it makes sense that the Lord would have classifications or ranks in His army, just as we have in our military system.

### 1.  Angel of the Lord

The *Angel of the Lord* has characteristics that set him apart from the other angels. First, he has the power to pardon or retain transgressions, and he carries the very name of God:

> *Behold, I send an Angel before you to keep you in the way and to bring you into the place which I have prepared. Beware of Him and obey His voice; do not provoke Him, for He will not pardon your transgressions; for My name is in Him* (Exodus 23:20-21).

Second, while God's character is revealed in him, through His name, he also reveals the face of God: *And He said, "My Presence* [literally, my face] *will go with you, and I will give you rest"* (Exodus 33:14).

Though he is called *God, the Angel of God,* and *the God of Bethel* (Genesis 31:11, 13), the Angel of the Lord is distinct from God (Zechariah 1:12-13).

Because of these characteristics, we can conclude that this is not a created angel, but the Son of God—the Messiah—a manifestation of Christ in the Old Testament, known as a *Christophany*.

## 2. The Archangel

An *Archangel* is a prince of angels. *Michael* is referred to as the archangel or chief angel (Jude 9). His name means "who is like God," and he stands up for the people of Israel in their defense:

> *At that time Michael shall stand up, The great prince who stands watch over the sons of your people; And there shall be a time of trouble, Such as never was since there was a nation, Even to that time. And at that time your people shall be delivered, Every one who is found written in the book* (Daniel 12:1).

Michael is considered the Prince of Israel: *But I will tell you what is noted in the Scripture of Truth. (No one upholds me against these, except Michael your prince)* (Daniel 10:21).

It was Michael and his angels who fought against Satan and his angels and cast them out of heaven when they rebelled against God:

> *And war broke out in heaven: Michael and his angels fought with the dragon; and the dragon and his angels fought, but they did not prevail, nor was a place found for*

> *them in heaven any longer. So the great dragon was cast out, that serpent of old, called the Devil and Satan, who deceives the whole world; he was cast to the earth, and his angels were cast out with him* (Revelation 12:7-9).

Also, Michael will come with Jesus at the Second Coming of the Lord:

> *For the Lord Himself will descend from heaven with a shout, with the voice of an archangel, and with the trumpet of God. And the dead in Christ will rise first* (1 Thessalonians 4:16).

While *Gabriel,* which means "the mighty one," is not referred to as an archangel, he holds a preeminent position as indicated in Luke 1:19: *And the angel answered and said to him, "I am Gabriel, who stands in the presence of God, and was sent to speak to you and bring you these glad tidings."*

He stands in the presence of God and is mentioned four times in the Bible, always as a bearer of good tidings concerning God's purposes and His kingdom, in connection with Christ:

> a. He informed Daniel of end times events (Daniel 8:15-27).
> b. He revealed the meaning of the seventy weeks to Daniel (Daniel 9:20-27).
> c. He spoke to Zacharias the priest about the coming of his son, John the Baptist (Luke 1:13, 19).
> d. He announced the birth of Jesus Christ, the Coming Messiah, to Mary, His mother (Luke 1:26-38).

## 3. Angels of the Nations

In the Book of Daniel, we see that there are guardian *angels of the nations* of the world. When Daniel was fasting and praying for the nation of Israel, an angel appeared to give him a message from the Throne of God. The angel explained that he had been delayed three weeks because of a battle waged by the Prince of Persia. This was not a physical battle, but a spiritual battle, so the prince was not a physical being, but a spiritual being or angel:

> *But the prince of the kingdom of Persia withstood me* [the angel] *twenty-one days; and behold, Michael, one of the chief princes, came to help me, for I had been left alone there with the kings of Persia* (Daniel 10:13).

However, the Archangel Michael, came to assist the messenger angel, allowing him to deliver his message to Daniel.

Later, as the angel left, he told Daniel that he was returning to the battle where the prince of Persia would be joined by the prince of Greece:

> *Then he said, "Do you know why I have come to you? And now I must return to fight with the prince of Persia; and when I have gone forth, indeed the prince of Greece will come"* (Daniel 10:20).

In the New Testament, the term *principalities* is used in reference to these "angels of the nations." They can be either good or bad angels:

> *I* [Paul] *should preach among the Gentiles the unsearchable riches of Chirst, . . . to the intent that now the manifold wisdom of God might be made known by the church to the principalities and powers in the heavenly places* (Ephesians 3:8,10).

> *Having disarmed principalities and powers, He made a public spectacle of them, triumphing over them in it* (Colossians 2:15).

> *For we do not wrestle against flesh and blood, but against principalities, against powers, against the rulers of the darkness of this age, against spiritual hosts of wickedness in the heavenly places* (Ephesians 6:12).

### 4. Cherubim

First mentioned in the Garden of Eden, the *Cherubim* are believed to be a part of God's justice towards man (Genesis 3:24), and redemption for man (Exodus 25:22):

*So He drove out the man; and He placed cherubim at the east of the garden of Eden, and a flaming sword which turned every way, to guard the way to the tree of life* (Genesis 3:24).

*And there I will meet with you, and I will speak with you from above the mercy seat, from between the two cherubim which are on the ark of the Testimony, about everything which I will give you in commandment to the children of Israel* (Exodus 25:22).

Cherubim are not only found in the Garden of Eden, but around the Throne of God (Psalm 99:1). Because of their position, they are connected with the righteousness and majesty of the throne of God. This is seen in the command of God to mount two golden Cherubim on the mercy seat, over the Ark of the Covenant in the Holy of Holies of the Tabernacle:

*He made two cherubim of beaten gold; he made them of one piece at the two ends of the mercy seat: one cherub at one end on this side, and the other cherub at the other end on that side. He made the cherubim at the two ends of one piece with the mercy seat. The cherubim spread out their wings above, and covered the mercy seat with their wings. They faced one another; the faces of the cherubim were toward the mercy seat* (Exodus 37:7-9).

God also had the Cherubim woven into the inner veil of the Tabernacle and Temple:

*Moreover you shall make the tabernacle with ten curtains of fine woven linen and blue, purple, and scarlet thread;*

*with artistic designs of cherubim you shall weave them* (Exodus 26:1).

We are not left to imagine the appearance of the Cherubim. Ezekiel leaves us with a very detailed description of these angels he saw descend from the firmament or heaven:

> *Each one had four faces, and each one had four wings. Their legs were straight, and the soles of their feet were like the soles of calves' feet. They sparkled like the color of burnished bronze. The hands of a man were under their wings on their four sides; and each of the four had faces and wings. Their wings touched one another. The creatures did not turn when they went, but each one went straight forward. As for the likeness of their faces, each had the face of a man; each of the four had the face of a lion on the right side, each of the four had the face of an ox on the left side, and each of the four had the face of an eagle* (Ezekiel 1:6-10; see also Ezekiel 10:1-22).

The four faces are believed to represent the most perfect of creation in: *strength*, the lion; *intelligence*, the man; *speed*, the eagle; and *service*, the ox.

### 5.  Seraphim

The word *Seraphim* means "the burning ones," and many believe their name represents their burning love for God. Throughout the entire Bible, they are only mentioned in Isaiah 6 and are found standing above the Throne of God. They have six wings and they praise God constantly:

> *Above it stood seraphim; each one had six wings: with two he covered his face, with two he covered his feet, and with two he flew. And one cried to another and said: "Holy, holy, holy is the LORD of hosts; The whole earth is full of His glory!"* (Isaiah 6:2-3).

# D. The Character and Attributes of Angels

It is important to look at the character and attributes of the angels because they are such a great example to us. As sinful man, we are willful and rebellious by nature whereas holy angels seek the will of God. By examining the character of the angels, we can learn how to be obedient, reverent, wise, meek, mighty and holy—all attributes of the angels of God.

### 1. Obedient

Unlike man, angels are obedient. They complete their tasks without hesitation and without complaint. That is the reason we pray, *Your will be done On earth as it is in heaven* (Matthew 6:10).

In heaven, the angels do not question the will of God: *Bless the LORD, all you His hosts, You ministers of His, who do His pleasure* (Psalm 103:21).

### 2. Reverent

The primary responsibility for an angel is to worship God. We see this throughout the Scriptures from the Old Testament to the New Testament:

> *You alone are the LORD; You have made heaven, The heaven of heavens, with all their host, The earth and everything on it, The seas and all that is in them, And You preserve them all. The host of heaven worships You* (Nehemiah 9:6).

> *But when He again brings the firstborn into the world, He says: "Let all the angels of God worship Him"* (Hebrews 1:6).

### 3. Wise

The wisdom of angels is finite, yet greater than man in his earthly, physical state. They are not infinite in wisdom like God, but they are able to discern between good and evil.

We see this when the woman of Tekoa said to the king:

> *"Your maidservant said, 'The word of my lord the king will now be comforting; for as the angel of God, so is my lord the king in discerning good and evil. And may the LORD your God be with you'"* (2 Samuel 14:17).

### 4. Meek

Unlike man, angels do not hold a grudge against one another, nor do they try to avenge themselves against an enemy (2 Peter 2:11). Even when Michael the Archangel opposed Satan for possession of Moses' body, he did not speak an accusation against him. Instead, he called upon the name of the Lord:

> *Yet Michael the archangel, in contending with the devil, when he disputed about the body of Moses, dared not bring against him a reviling accusation, but said, "The Lord rebuke you!"* (Jude 9).

### 5. Mighty

The angels are mighty in strength. One angel destroyed one hundred and eighty-five thousand Assyrian soldiers in a single night:

> *And it came to pass on a certain night that the angel of the LORD went out, and killed in the camp of the Assyrians one hundred and eighty-five thousand; and when people arose early in the morning, there were the corpses; all dead* (2 Kings 19:35).

### 6. Holy

Angels have been created by God, set apart by God, for God and are *holy* angels:

> *When the Son of Man comes in His glory, and all the holy angels with Him, then He will sit on the throne of His glory* (Matthew 25:31).

How many attributes or characteristics do you share with the angels of heaven? I can see where I fall short, but it does not discourage me—it encourages me to seek God more and more, as I pursue His perfect will for my life. I realize that I must die to my will and seek His will in order to obtain godly character.

## E. The Ministry of Angels in Heaven

The principal and most important ministry of angels in heaven is worshipping and offering unceasing praise to God:

> *Then I looked, and I heard the voice of many angels around the throne, the living creatures, and the elders; and the number of them was ten thousand times ten thousand, and thousands of thousands, saying with a loud voice: "Worthy is the Lamb who was slain To receive power and riches and wisdom, And strength and honor and glory and blessing!" And every creature which is in heaven and on the earth and under the earth and such as are in the sea, and all that are in them, I heard saying: "Blessing and honor and glory and power Be to Him who sits on the throne, And to the Lamb, forever and ever!" Then the four living creatures said, "Amen!" And the twenty-four elders fell down and worshiped Him who lives forever and ever* (Revelation 5:11-14).

> *Then another angel, having a golden censer, came and stood at the altar. He was given much incense, that he should offer it with the prayers of all the saints upon the golden altar which was before the throne. And the smoke of the incense, with the prayers of the saints, ascended before God from the angel's hand* (Revelation 8:3-4).

In the Book of Revelation, we can see the many duties of angels as they minster at the throne in praise and worship, gather the church at the Second Coming of Christ, announce the judgments of God, pour out the wrath of God, assist on the Day of Judgment and stand at the gates of the New Jerusalem.

## F. The Ministry of Angels on Earth

Angels have three ministries here on earth. They are used as *God's agents*, *His messengers*, and *His servants*. In each of these ministries, God uses His angels to come alongside of us and help us in our individual walks with the Lord.

### God's Agents

As *God's agents*, angels execute His judgments:

> *Two angels came to Sodom in the evening . . . "For we will destroy this place, because the outcry against them has grown great before the face of the LORD, and the LORD has sent us to destroy it"* (Genesis 19:1, 13).

> *And when the angel stretched out His hand over Jerusalem to destroy it, the LORD relented from the destruction, and said to the angel who was destroying the people, "It is enough; now restrain your hand." And the angel of the LORD was by the threshing floor of Araunah the Jebusite* (2 Samuel 24:16).

> *For the Son of Man will come in the glory of His Father with His angels, and then He will reward each according to his works* (Matthew 16:27).

> *Then immediately an angel of the Lord struck him [Herod], because he did not give glory to God. And he was eaten by worms and died* (Acts 12:23).

### God's Messengers

As *God's messengers*, angels communicate:

1. **Announcements**
   > *But while he thought about these things, behold, an angel of the Lord appeared to him in a dream, saying, "Joseph, son of David, do not be afraid to take to you Mary your wife, for that which is conceived in her is of the Holy Spirit. And she will bring forth a Son, and you shall call His name JESUS, for He will save His people from their sins"* (Matthew 1:20-21).

2. **Warnings**

   *Now when they had departed, behold, an angel of the Lord appeared to Joseph in a dream, saying, "Arise, take the young Child and His mother, flee to Egypt, and stay there until I bring you word; for Herod will seek the young Child to destroy Him"* (Matthew 2:13).

3. **Instruction**

   *Yes, while I was speaking in prayer, the man Gabriel, whom I had seen in the vision at the beginning, being caused to fly swiftly, reached me about the time of the evening offering. And he informed me, and talked with me, and said, "O Daniel, I have now come forth to give you skill to understand"* (Daniel 9:21-22).

4. **Encouragement**

   *"For there stood by me this night an angel of the God to whom I belong and whom I serve, saying, 'Do not be afraid, Paul; you must be brought before Caesar; and indeed God has granted you all those who sail with you' "* (Acts 27:23-24).

### God's Ministering Servants

As *God's servants*, angels are sent to minister to us, who are heirs of salvation (Hebrews 1:14). They do so in the following ways:

1. **They Sustain**

   *Then an angel appeared to Him from heaven, strengthening Him* (Luke 22:43).

2. **They Preserve**

   *Behold, I send an Angel before you to keep you in the way and to bring you into the place which I have prepared* (Exodus 23:20).

3. **They Deliver**

   *The angel of the LORD encamps all around those who fear Him, And delivers them* (Psalm 34:7; see also 2 Kings 6:16-17).

4. **They Intercede**
   *Then the Angel of the LORD answered and said, "O LORD of hosts, how long will You not have mercy on Jerusalem and on the cities of Judah, against which You were angry these seventy years?"* (Zechariah 1:12).

5. **They Minister to us after We Die**
   *So it was that the beggar died, and was carried by the angels to Abraham's bosom. The rich man also died and was buried* (Luke 16:22).

6. **They Rejoice at our Salvation**
   *Likewise, I say to you, there is joy in the presence of the angels of God over one sinner who repents* (Luke 15:10).

# G. The Ranking and Function of Angels

According to the Scriptures, there is a multitude of angels (Hebrews 12:22). The writers of the Word could not declare their sum. John described the vast amount of angels around the throne of God like this:

*Then I looked, and I heard the voice of many angels around the throne, the living creatures, and the elders; and the number of them was ten thousand times ten thousand, and thousands of thousands* (Revelation 5:11).

As I said before, God is a God of order, so with such a multitude of angels, we see a type of ranking among them. This rank and hierarchy is not limited only to the angels in heaven, but Satan also uses similar ranking with the fallen angels.

Some of the ranks of the good angels are described in Ephesians 1:21 where Christ is seated, *far above all principality and power and might and dominion, and every name that is named, not only in this age but also in that which is to come.*

The same ranking system is reflected in reference to the fallen angels in Ephesians 6:12:

*For we do not wrestle against flesh and blood, but against principalities, against powers, against the rulers of the darkness of this age, against spiritual hosts of wickedness in the heavenly places.*

No one can say for certain the exact hierarchy, but the functions and ranks of the angels can be identified:

### 1.  Thrones

First, *thrones* refer to the angels that are in the immediate presence of the Lord. These angels are symbols of God's justice and authority and are believed to be the most spiritually perfect of all angels:

*For by Him all things were created that are in heaven and that are on earth, visible and invisible, whether thrones or dominions or principalities or powers. All things were created through Him and for Him* (Colossians 1:16).

### 2.  Dominions

Second, there are *dominions*. In the Jewish and the Christian hierarchies of angels (Ezekiel 1:4), they are also known as *hashmallim,* referring to their radiant amber appearance. These angels are known to rule over nations, and also control the duties of the lower angels: *And all dominions shall serve and obey Him* (Daniel 7:27).

### 3.  Principalites and Authorities

Third, p*rincipalities* and *authorities* are beings who exercise imperial responsibility and power. They are seen as "princes" serving under angels of superior rank. The following verses show principalities in the ranks of angels, and also in the ranks of demons:

*The manifold wisdom of God might be made known by the church to the principalities and powers in the heavenly places* (Ephesians 3:10).

*Jesus Christ who has gone into heaven and is at the right hand of God, angels and authorities and powers having been made subject to Him* (1 Peter 3:22).

*Having disarmed principalities and powers, He* [Christ] *made a public spectacle of them, triumphing over them in it* (Colossians 2:15).

## 4. Might

Fourth, "angels over celestial bodies" are referred to as *might*. They are called this because of their powerful nature. Their primary purpose is to supervise the movements of the heavenly bodies, so that the universe remains in order. Christ is seated, *far above all principality and power and might and dominion, and every name that is named, not only in this age but also in that which is to come* (Ephesians 1:21).

## 5. Powers

Fifth, *powers* are ranks of warrior angels who were created to be completely loyal to God. It is believed that powers have never fallen from grace. They oversee the distribution of power among humans:

*For I am persuaded that neither death nor life, nor angels nor principalities nor powers, nor things present nor things to come . . . shall be able to separate us from the love of God which is in Christ Jesus our Lord* (Romans 8:38).

*You are complete in Him, who is the head of all principality and power* (Colossians 2:10).

As we study the various ranks of the angels, we again see God's perfect creation. Nothing God created was done in chaos and disarray, but in perfect goodness and order, from the creation of the world to the creation of man and everything in between.

## Chapter 10

# DOCTRINE OF SATAN & DEMONS
# SATANOLOGY
# DEMONOLOGY

## A. Satan

1. Satan's Origin
2. Satan's Character
3. Satan's Names
    a. Satan
    b. Devil
    c. Tempter
    d. Serpent
    e. Destroyer
    f. Prince or Ruler of this World
    g. Murderer
    h. Father of Lies
4. Satan's Activity
5. Satan's Final Destiny

## B. Demons

1. The Origin of Demons
2. The Ranks of Demons
3. The Power of Demons
4. Demons and False Doctrine
5. Demon Possession
6. The Final Destiny of Demons

# Doctrine of Satan & Demons
## SATANOLOGY
Hebrew word: *satan* means, "opponent"
Greek word: *Satanas* means "the accuser"

## DEMONOLOGY
Greek word: *daimonion* means "a demonic being," a demon.

*So the great dragon was cast out, that serpent of old, called the Devil and Satan, who deceives the whole world; he was cast to the earth, and his angels were cast out with him* (Revelation 12:9).

The Bible speaks of a spiritual realm in which both angels and demons exist:

*For we do not wrestle against flesh and blood, but against principalities, against powers, against the rulers of the darkness of this age, against spiritual hosts of wickedness in the heavenly places* (Ephesians 6:12).

Satan and his demons not only exist in hell, but we wrestle against them here on earth. I learned as a Marine, it is always best to know your enemies; make no mistake, Satan and his demons are very real enemies of man.

## A. Satan
Know your enemy. Some have said that Satan is not real, but is just a figure of speech, or should be viewed in a metaphorical sense. His existence is usually challenged by those who deny the supernatural or spiritual realm. The Bible emphatically describes the existence of Satan as a real being, and what is said about him is to be taken literally.

## 1. Satan's Origin

When we think of Satan or the Devil, we often picture a hideous, grotesque being with horns, cloven feet and a pitch fork. You might even think he is red—isn't that how all the cartoons depict him?

In reality, Satan was originally *Lucifer*, "the light-bearer." That is why he often appears to us as an *angel of light* (2 Corinthians 11:14). It is believed that he was one of the most beautiful of all God's angels. Perhaps, because of his great beauty, he aspired to be greater than God.

In his aspiration to be worshipped and set above God, he allowed pride and envy to take a hold of his heart and bring him down. He is the ultimate example to us that the sin of pride leads to nothing more than total destruction (Ezekiel 28:12-19).

Because Satan is an angel, he was created by God and was a servant of God. He was not just a servant, but many believe he may have been the choir director in heaven, leading the angels in their worship of God.

However, Satan allowed the sin of pride to take control of his life, and he was cast out of heaven along with his rebellious followers. Isaiah, inspired by the Spirit of God, wrote about him:

> *"How you are fallen from heaven, O Lucifer, son of the morning! How you are cut down to the ground, You who weakened the nations! For you have said in your heart: 'I will ascend into heaven, I will exalt my throne above the stars of God; I will also sit on the mount of the congregation On the farthest sides of the north; I will ascend above the heights of the clouds, I will be like the Most High.' Yet you shall be brought down to Sheol, To the lowest depths of the Pit"* (Isaiah 14:12-15).

The Apostle John, forseeing the future, wrote:

> *So the great dragon was cast out, that serpent of old, called the Devil and Satan, who deceives the whole world; he was cast to the earth, and his angels were cast out with him* (Revelation 12:9).

## 2. Satan's Character

Satan is mentioned five times in the Old Testament and 72 times in the New Testament, which is more than any other person mentioned outside of God the Father, Jesus Christ, and the Holy Spirit. His character is revealed in the many titles used when referencing him throughout the Scriptures.

The Bible also attributes a personality to Satan by referring to him with personal pronouns, such as *he* and *him*. It also describes him as having a will, an intellect and knowledge, as well as emotions of anger, jealousy and hatred.

## 3. Satan's Names

Many different names are attributed to him throughout the Bible, which include: Satan, Devil, Tempter, Serpent or Dragon, Destroyer, Prince of this World, Murderer and Father of Lies. Each of these names reveals his evil nature.

### a. Satan

*Satan* means "adversary." As an adversary of God, he is always trying to put road blocks in the path of God's plan. From the very beginning, he tried to stop the coming of a Messiah by deceiving Eve (Genesis 3:15).

He also tries to destroy the church, using people within the church who are false teachers (1 Timothy 4:1) and people outside the church who persecute the believers (Revelation 2:10).

### b. Devil

*Devil* means "slanderer." Satan slandered God by accusing Him of lying (Genesis 3:2, 4-5). Satan slandered Job by accusing him before God (Job 1:6-11). As the *accuser of the brethren* (Revelation 12:10), Satan is out to slander each one of us.

### c. Tempter

*Tempter* speaks of how he comes to test or try us. We should expect him to tempt us as he did with Jesus in the wilderness: *Now when the tempter came to Him, he said, "If You are the Son of God, command that these stones become bread"* (Matthew 4:3). He tempted Jesus to come against God the Father. While God tests us to build character, Satan tempts us to destroy our lives. In every temptation, God provides a means of escape; we do not have to give in (Matthew 6:13; 1 Corinthians 10:13).

### d. Serpent

Satan is that *serpent of old*. When we look back to the beginning of time, we see that he came to Eve in the Garden of Eden and deceived her, leading her to sin against God (Genesis 3:1-5). This title brings such a vivid picture to mind when I read it: *that serpent of old, called the Devil and Satan* (Revelation 12:9).

### e. Destroyer

In the Book of Revelation, the title of *destroyer* is given to Satan: *And they had as king over them the angel of the bottomless pit, whose name in Hebrew is Abaddon, but in Greek he has the name Apollyon* (Revelation 9:11). *Abaddon* and *Apollyon* both mean "destroyer." During the Tribulation, Satan is let out of the pit and allowed to torment the people for five months (Revelation 9:5). Destroying people's lives is Satan's ultimate goal. He wants to do more than steal or kill.

He wants the total destruction of each individual: *The thief does not come except to steal, and to kill, and to destroy* (John 10:10).

### f.   Prince or Ruler of this World

*Prince* or *Ruler of this world* expresses Satan's influence over this world in opposition to the will of God (1 John 5:19). However, we see in John 12:31 that he will not be allowed to hold onto this title: *Now is the judgment of this world; now the ruler of this world will be cast out.* God will cast him down and take him off his throne.

### g.   Murderer

Jesus revealed that Satan *was a murderer from the beginning* (John 8:44; see also 1 John 3:12).

### h.   Father of Lies

Jesus further tells us that Satan is the *Father of lies* in John 8:44, *and does not stand in the truth, because there is no truth in him. When he speaks a lie, he speaks from his own resources, for he is a liar and the father of it.*

Regardless of the name or title used of Satan, it is clear that he is consumed with pride and hate. His main goal with man is to hurt him. There are numerous warnings throughout the Bible about Satan's attempt to deceive and destroy believers:

*Be sober, be vigilant; because your adversary the devil walks about like a roaring lion, seeking whom he may devour. Resist him, steadfast in the faith, knowing that the same sufferings are experienced by your brotherhood in the world* (1 Peter 5:8-9).

Satan is real and the Word of God strongly warns about him.

## 4. Satan's Activity

In all that he does, Satan has one ultimate goal—to oppose the work of God. In the process, he seeks to destroy man, who is the very image of God. No wonder he hates us so much. We represent God! He uses all his wiles as tempter, deceiver, destroyer, accuser, liar, and the list goes on, to come against God and His people: *But I* [Paul] *fear, lest somehow, as the serpent deceived Eve by his craftiness, so your minds may be corrupted from the simplicity that is in Christ* (2 Corinthians 11:3).

He not only uses the wicked to come against God and the church, but he even attempts to cause division and dissention among believers—to bring down the church. Satan is very clever and crafty. In 2 Corinthians 11:14, we learn that he can disguise himself to deceive God's people: *And no wonder! For Satan himself transforms himself into an angel of light.*

In Job, we see that Satan roams the earth, and he was very well informed about the character and possessions of Job. He had been very busy, at some point, studying the life of Job: *And the LORD said to Satan, "From where do you come?" So Satan answered the LORD and said, "From going to and fro on the earth, and from walking back and forth on it"* (Job 1:7).

Since he is not all knowing or omniscient, as only God is, he studies us to find out all our weaknesses. The Scriptures warn us to be diligent and serious regarding Satan and his mission to destroy us. Very often, he uses our own weaknesses to bring about our destruction: *Be sober, be vigilant; because your adversary the devil walks about like a roaring lion, seeking whom he may devour* (1 Peter 5:8).

## 5. Satan's Final Destiny

You may be thinking you are outmatched by Satan. Before you get discouraged, thinking you can never overcome the temptations and wiles of the enemy, remember, the victory has already been won! Jesus defeated Satan on the cross.

From the very beginning, in the Book of Genesis, God told us Satan would fail: *"And I will put enmity Between you* [the serpent] *and the woman, And between your seed and her Seed; He shall bruise your head, And you shall bruise His heel"* (Genesis 3:15).

Satan began his existence in heaven, as Lucifer, a luminous angel of God, but was cast down to earth: *I* [the Son of God] *saw Satan fall like lightning from heaven* (Luke 10:18).

The good news is that when Christ was put on the cross for our sins, He won the victory over Satan and our foes:

> *Having disarmed principalities and powers, He* [Christ] *made a public spectacle of them, triumphing over them in it* (Colossians 2:15).

> *He who is in you* [Christ] *is greater than he* [Satan] *who is in the world* (1 John 4:4b).

> *If God is for us, who can be against us?* (Romans 8:31b).

Always keep in mind; it is through Christ that victory has been won. We cannot face Satan in our own strength. The only power we possess is through the cross of Jesus Christ. We must put on the armor of God: *Put on the whole armor of God, that you may be able to stand against the wiles of the devil* (Ephesians 6:11).

When Jesus sets up His kingdom in the Millennium, Satan will be bound for 1,000 years. At the end of the Millennium, he is released and will make one final attempt to come against God. After his final defeat by Christ, he will be cast into the Lake of Fire: *The devil, who deceived them, was cast into the lake of fire and brimstone where the beast and the false prophet are. And they will be tormented day and night forever and ever* (Revelation 20:10).

There will be no second chances. This will be Satan's final destination and defeat—separated from God in utter darkness—for eternity!

## B. Demons

Since Satan cannot be everywhere all the time, omnipresent like God, he relies on demons to help him in his opposition of God's work and His church.

As followers of Satan, they share his desire to oppose God's purposes, and Satan uses them to execute his plans and purpose:

> *Then he* [an angelic being] *said to me, "Do not fear, Daniel, for from the first day that you set your heart to understand, and to humble yourself before your God, your words were heard; and I have come because of your words. But the prince of the kingdom of Persia* [Satan, the power of the Persian leader] *withstood me twenty-one days; and behold, Michael, one of the chief princes, came to help me, for I had been left alone there with the kings of Persia* [demonic beings]. *Now I have come to make you understand what will happen to your people in the latter days, for the vision refers to many days yet to come"* (Daniel 10:12-14).

### 1.  The Origin of Demons

Because God proclaimed that everything He created was good (Genesis 1:31), and He created everything, we can determine that demons are fallen angels, created perfect by God, who possess the power of free will—just like good angels and man. They freely chose to sin and follow Satan in his rebellion against God and were cast out of heaven: *For if God did not spare the angels who sinned, but cast them down to hell and delivered them into chains of darkness, to be reserved for judgment* (2 Peter 2:4).

### 2.  The Ranks of Demons

Just as the angels of God have ranks, the Bible tells of the *ranks* of the demons who work for Satan. Many of the angelic ranks are countered by demonic ranks. As you study them, you will see a similarity to the duties of some of the angels, but with evil intent. High ranking demons develop strategy and tactics while directing the activities of fallen angels:

> "And I [Jesus] *also say to you that you are*
> *Peter, and on this rock I will build My church, and*
> *the gates of Hades* [Hell] *shall not prevail against it"*
> (Matthew 16:18).

Jesus' use of the term *the gates of Hades* describes the authority exercised by demons. The main gate of a city was the place where the leading authorities and judges of that city met, conducted and exercised their official authority. Jesus used this term when describing demonic authority.

Ephesians 6:12 refers to other ranks of demons, such as *principalities, powers, rulers of darkness* and *spiritual hosts of wickedness*. First, there are the *rulers of darkness* of this world. They are demons that rule over nations and control the duties of the lower ranking demons.

Next, there are *principalities* and *powers*. These demons possess great responsibility and power. Last, are the *spiritual hosts of wickedness*. This rank encompasses the host of fallen angels.

### 3.  The Power of Demons
Demons, as spiritual beings, are stronger and more powerful than man, with the ability to afflict the children of God and even hinder our spiritual walk with the Lord.

Jesus said:
> "So ought not this woman, being a daughter of Abraham,
> whom Satan has bound—think of it—for eighteen years,
> be loosed from this bond on the Sabbath?" (Luke 13:16).

> For we do not wrestle against flesh and blood,
> but against principalities, against powers, against the
> rulers of the darkness of this age, against spiritual hosts of
> wickedness in the heavenly places (Ephesians 6:12).

However, in their greatest power, they are no match for Jesus. It is God who is all powerful, omnipotent, not Satan and not his demons. In every encounter Jesus had with the demons, we can see their fear of Him and His power: *And suddenly they* [demons] *cried out, saying, "What have we to do with You, Jesus, You Son of God? Have You come here to torment us before the time?"* (Matthew 8:29).

The demons fear God, not man, so we must be aware of the power they possess. Remember, the only power we have against demons is through the name of Jesus Christ (Acts 16:18). Demons desire to afflict Christians and cause us to be weak in our spiritual walk, but by knowing their strength and their strategies, we are able to withstand the wiles of the enemy:

> *Therefore take up the whole armor of God, that you may be able to withstand in the evil day, and having done all, to stand. Stand therefore, having girded your waist with truth, having put on the breastplate of righteousness, and having shod your feet with the preparation of the gospel of peace; above all, taking the shield of faith with which you will be able to quench all the fiery darts of the wicked one. And take the helmet of salvation, and the sword of the Spirit, which is the word of God; praying always with all prayer and supplication in the Spirit, being watchful to this end with all perseverance and supplication for all the saints* (Ephesians 6:13-18).

## 4. Demons and False Doctrine

Paul warns us that in the last days, demons will deceive people into believing false doctrine:

> *Now the Spirit expressly says that in latter times some will depart from the faith, giving heed to deceiving spirits and doctrines of demons, speaking lies in hypocrisy, having their own conscience seared with a hot iron* (1 Timothy 4:1-2).

You may think you could never be deceived by some false teaching. You may believe that you know God's Word so well, nothing could get past you. However, in Matthew 24:24, Christ warns us, *"For false christs and false prophets will rise and show great signs and wonders to deceive, if possible, even the elect."* As God's people, we are the targets of false teachers and their false doctrines.

## 5. Demon Possession

I want to be emphatically clear that Christians cannot be demon possessed. If you are filled with the Holy Spirit, you cannot be possessed by a demon. The Bible says in 1 Corinthians 6:19, *Or do you not know that your body is the temple of the Holy Spirit who is in you.*

It is so important to remember that God is much more powerful than Satan and his demons (Romans 8:31, 38-39). We should never give them more authority or power than they actually possess (1 John 4:4).

It is also important to remember that Satan's greatest desire is to deceive and destroy believers by drawing us away from God and His Word (2 Corinthians 11:3). When his demons deceive people, they are able to not only draw them away from God, but cause them to do things contrary to the teaching of Jesus—causing further separation from God and His truth:

> *Rather, that the things which the Gentiles sacrifice they sacrifice to demons and not to God, and I do not want you to have fellowship with demons. You cannot drink the cup of the Lord and the cup of demons; you cannot partake of the Lord's table and of the table of demons* (1 Corinthians 10:20-21).

Satan loves to counterfeit the works of God in many ways; demon possession is an evil representation of the indwelling of the Holy Spirit. As Christians are transformed by the indwelling of the Holy Spirit, with their speech and conduct under the influence of the Spirit, so it is for the unbeliever when they are indwelt with a demon. They are under the influence of the demon, saying and doing things they would not normally do:

*Then one was brought to Him who was demon-possessed, blind and mute; and He healed him, so that the blind and mute man both spoke and saw* (Matthew 12:22).

*And often he* [a demon] *has thrown him both into the fire and into the water to destroy him. But if You can do anything, have compassion on us and help us* (Mark 9:22).

In some cases, more than one demon takes possession of a body:

*Jesus asked him, saying, "What is your name?" And he said, "Legion," because many demons had entered him* (Luke 8:30).

*And certain women who had been healed of evil spirits and infirmities; Mary called Magdalene, out of whom had come seven demons* (Luke 8:2).

While Satan would like to imitate what God does, what he offers is always a cheap imitation. When we are indwelt by the Holy Spirit, we still have the power to exercise our own free will. We can allow the Holy Spirit to guide us, or we can allow the flesh to guide us. When an unbeliever is possessed, they no longer have control of their actions. They are bound and unable to free themselves from their demon possession. Demons can only be cast out of a person by the name of Jesus Christ: *But Paul, greatly annoyed, turned and said to the spirit, "I command you in the name of Jesus Christ to come out of her." And he came out that very hour* (Acts 16:18).

In some cases, fasting is also required. In Matthew 17:14-21, the Apostles were unable to cast out the demon from a young child, and Jesus told them, *"However, this kind* [of demon] *does not go out except by prayer and fasting"* (Matthew 17:21).

We must always keep in mind that we do not have the power to cast out demons on our own. Jesus gave the Apostles power to cast out demons and heal the sick, and it is only in His name that we have any power:

> *And when He had called His twelve disciples to Him, He gave them power over unclean spirits, to cast them out, and to heal all kinds of sickness and all kinds of disease* (Matthew 10:1).

> *And He said to them, "Behold, I give you the authority to trample on serpents and scorpions, and over all the power of the enemy, and nothing shall by any means hurt you. Nevertheless do not rejoice in this, that the spirits are subject to you, but rather rejoice because your names are written in heaven"* (Luke 10:18-20).

In dealing with a demon possessed individual, I cannot stress more how we must be right before the Lord when we approach such a person (Acts 19:13-15). While in possession of a human, the demons find rest and satisfaction, so immediately after they have been cast out, they look for a person to possess. Jesus said in Matthew 12:43-45:

> *"When an unclean spirit goes out of a man, he goes through dry places, seeking rest, and finds none. Then he says, 'I will return to my house from which I came.' And when he comes, he finds it empty, swept, and put in order. Then he goes and takes with him seven other spirits more wicked than himself, and they enter and dwell there; and the last state of that man is worse than the first. So shall it also be with this wicked generation."*

Not only must we be clean before the Lord when dealing with demons, but the possessed person must get their life right with the Lord once the demon or demons have been cast out or risk another demon possession—possibly worse than the first.

I must warn you, there are things we can get involved with that open the door to Satan and his demons, making us vulnerable to demon oppression. As Christians, we should never get involved with the occult, witchcraft, astrology, tarot cards, Ouija boards, drugs or anything associated with cultic rituals. These are not harmless activities. By participating in these activities, you open the door for Satan to harass you.

I do not want to leave you with fear. As Christians, we possess the most powerful weapon against demons, and that is the indwelling of the Holy Spirit: *If God is for us, who can be against us?* (Romans 8:31). We are not to go out of our way to look for demons, but when we encounter them, we do not have to be afraid (1 John 4:4).

## 6. The Final Destiny of Demons
Yes, demons are a powerful group—harassing, deceiving, causing afflictions and even possessing individuals— but as with Satan, we have victory through Christ Jesus (1 Corinthians 15:57). This victory exists now, not only in the last days.

As stated earlier, through His crucifixion, Christ won the victory over our foes and fully *disarmed principalities and powers, He made a public spectacle of them, triumphing over them in it* (Colossians 2:15).

Just like Satan, the fallen angels or demons are defeated foes, and they will be cast into the Lake of Fire, along with Satan:

> *"Then He* [Jesus] *will also say . . . 'Depart from Me, you cursed, into the everlasting fire prepared for the Devil and his angels' "* (Matthew 25:41).

# Chapter 11

## DOCTRINE OF THE LAST THINGS

## ESCHATOLOGY

### A. Death

Terms for Death

1. Sleep
2. Departing
3. Yielding Up the Spirit
4. Fading Away
5. Going Down Into Silence
6. Gathered to Your People
7. God Requiring Your Soul
8. Returning to the Dust

### B. The Resurrection

1. Nature of the Resurrection
2. Eternity
3. The First Resurrection: Righteous
4. The Second Resurrection: Unrighteous

### C. The Destiny of the Righteous

### D. The Destiny of the Wicked

### E. The Order of the Last Things

### F. The Rapture

## G. The Tribulation
1.  The Unholy Trinity
2.  The Abomination of Desolation
3.  God's Judgments

## H. The Second Coming of Jesus Christ
1.  What is the Second Coming?
2.  The Time of the Second Coming of Christ
3.  The Purpose for the Second Coming

## I.  The Millennium

## J.  The Judgment

## K. All Things Made New

# DOCTRINE OF THE LAST THINGS
# ESCHATOLOGY
Greek words: *eschatos* means "last," and
*ology* comes from *logos* which means "subject matter"

*Jesus said, "And behold, I am coming quickly, and My reward is with Me, to give to every one according to his work. I am the Alpha and the Omega, the Beginning and the End, the First and the Last"* (Revelation 22:12-13).

## A. Death

For many people, *death* is a scary thing, but death is not the end of our existence—it is only "the separation of the body and the soul." It is a transition from our physical or earthly existence to our spiritual existence. This transition takes us from our mortal existence into immortality, as we shed our mortal bodies and move into the spiritual realm. As Christians, we should not fear death. Paul said in Philippians 1:21: *For to me, to live is Christ, and to die is gain.*

### Terms for Death
#### 1. Sleep
John 11:11, *These things He* [Jesus] *said, and after that He said to them, "Our friend Lazarus sleeps, but I go that I may wake him up"* (see also 1 Thessalonians 4:13-18; 1 Corinthians 15:51-52).

#### 2. Departing
Philippians 1:23, *For I* [Paul] *am hard pressed between the two, having a desire to depart and be with Christ, which is far better.*

#### 3. Yielding Up the Spirit
Matthew 27:50, *And Jesus cried out again with a loud voice, and yielded up His spirit.*

### 4. Fading Away

Job 14:2, *He* [man] *comes forth like a flower and fades away; He flees like a shadow and does not continue.*

### 5. Going Down Into Silence

Psalm 115:17, *The dead do not praise the LORD, Nor any who go down into silence.*

### 6. Gathered to Your People

Genesis 49:33, *And when Jacob had finished commanding his sons, he drew his feet up into the bed and breathed his last, and was gathered to his people.*

### 7. God Requiring Your Soul

Luke 12:20, Jesus spoke a parable saying, *"But God said to him, 'Fool! This night your soul will be required of you; then whose will those things be which you have provided?' "*

### 8. Returning to the Dust

Genesis 3:19, God said to Adam, *"In the sweat of your face you shall eat bread Till you return to the ground, For out of it you were taken; For dust you are, And to dust you shall return."*

In the previous verses, we see the transition, with the death of the physical body returning to the dust from which it was made (Genesis 2:7), as the spirit of the believer enters heaven with Christ (Luke 23:43; 2 Corinthians 5:1, 8), and the spirit of the unbeliever enters hell (Luke 16:22-23).

For the believer, death does not have the last word. While sin has its last effect on the believer, the sting of death has been taken away (1 Corinthians 15:55-56). By Christ's death and resurrection, we have been given eternal life, and death has no power over us. Our earthly bodies will perish and go back to the dust, but we will live forever:

> *Jesus said to her, "I am the resurrection and the life. He who believes in Me, though he may die, he shall live. And whoever*

*lives and believes in Me shall never die. Do you believe this?"*
(John 11:25-26).

Remember the words of Paul in Philippians 1:21, *to die is gain*.
What he means is that while this earthly body may die, it is all
the better because he will be with Christ, eternally.

## B. The Resurrection
### 1. Nature of the Resurrection
The truth and fact of the resurrection is supported scripturally
and taught in both the Old Testament and the New
Testament. There is no contradiction between the two; they
are in full agreement.

In the Old Testament, Job, in all his infirmities, expressed
how he was comforted by the knowledge of the resurrection
in Job 19:25-27:

> *"For I know that my Redeemer lives, And He shall stand
> at last on the earth; And after my skin is destroyed, this
> I know, That in my flesh I shall see God, Whom I shall
> see for myself, And my eyes shall behold, and not another.
> How my heart yearns within me!"*

In the New Testament, Paul wrote an entire chapter
to the church of Corinth concerning the resurrection,
1 Corinthians 15. He stressed the power of the resurrection
in 1 Corinthians 15:42-43:

> *So also is the resurrection of the dead. The body is sown
> in corruption, it is raised in incorruption. It is sown in
> dishonor, it is raised in glory. It is sown in weakness, it
> is raised in power.*

Paul also emphasized how Christ, our example in all things,
was the first resurrection in a glorified body in 1 Corinthians
15:20: *But now Christ is risen from the dead, and has become the
firstfruits of those who have fallen asleep* [died].

When Christ was resurrected, He did not have a corruptible body, but a glorified body—a body that passed through doors: *And after eight days His disciples were again inside, and Thomas with them. Jesus came, the doors being shut, and stood in the midst, and said, "Peace to you!"* (John 20:26).

His body was also solid to the touch: *Then He said to Thomas, "Reach your finger here, and look at My hands; and reach your hand here, and put it into My side. Do not be unbelieving, but believing"* (John 20:27).

One day, we will have glorified bodies like Jesus:

> *For our citizenship is in heaven, from which we also eagerly wait for the Savior, the Lord Jesus Christ, who will transform our lowly body that it may be conformed to His glorious body, according to the working by which He is able even to subdue all things to Himself* (Philippians 3:20-21).

While we cannot conceive of the glorified body and the difference between it and the body we now inhabit, we have the assurance of the Scriptures that it is an incorruptible body that will no longer experience pain and suffering. In Revelation 21:4, a loud voice from heaven declared, *"And God will wipe away every tear from their eyes; there shall be no more death, nor sorrow, nor crying. There shall be no more pain, for the former things have passed away."*

## 2. Eternity

We have already established that we will all taste of death. We will all die and pass from a temporal to an eternal existence, but not all will embrace eternal life. The believer will embrace the resurrection of life, basking in the very presence of Christ, while the unbeliever will be delivered to the resurrection of damnation, completely separated from the Lord, in eternal darkness: *And many of those who sleep in the dust of the earth shall awake, Some to everlasting life, Some to shame and everlasting contempt* (Daniel 12:2).

Thus there are two *resurrections*. The *first resurrection* is the "resurrection of the righteous." The second is the "resurrection of the unrighteous." In John 5:29, Jesus speaks of the two resurrections: *"and come forth; those who have done good, to the resurrection of life, and those who have done evil, to the resurrection of condemnation."*

Paul also mentions the resurrection of the just and unjust in Acts 24:15: *"I have hope in God, which they themselves also accept, that there will be a resurrection of the dead, both of the just and the unjust."*

### 3.  The First Resurrection: Righteous

The resurrection of the righteous is known as the *first resurrection* (Revelation 20:6). There are *three moments* or *events* in the resurrection of the righteous.

The first event occurred when Christ died and descended into *the lower parts of the earth* (Hades or hell), and released the righteous who were there in Abraham's bosom, bringing them to heaven with Him:

> *Therefore He says: "When He ascended on high, He led captivity captive, And gave gifts to men." (Now this, "He ascended"; what does it mean but that He also first descended into the lower parts of the earth? He who descended is also the One who ascended far above all the heavens, that He might fill all things)* (Ephesians 4:8-10).

The second event will occur at the *Rapture of the church.* Believers who have already died will rise first with Christ, and then the living believers will be caught up with Him:

> *For the Lord Himself will descend from heaven with a shout, with the voice of an archangel, and with the trumpet of God. And the dead in Christ will rise first. Then we who are alive and remain shall be caught up together with them in the clouds to meet the Lord in the air. And thus we shall always be with the Lord* (1 Thessalonians 4:16-17).

The third event will take place at the end of the Great Tribulation, when the *Tribulation saints will be resurrected* and will reign with Christ for 1000 years in the Millennium Kingdom:

> *Then I saw the souls of those who had been beheaded for their witness to Jesus and for the word of God, who had not worshiped the beast or his image, and had not received his mark on their foreheads or on their hands. And they lived and reigned with Christ for a thousand years* (Revelation 20:4).

### 4. The Second Resurrection: Unrighteous

Unbelievers will not be resurrected with the church at the coming of Jesus at the Rapture. They will be resurrected after the Millennial (1000 year) Reign of Christ: *But the rest of the dead did not live again until the thousand years were finished* (Revelation 20:5).

This is known as the *second resurrection,* the resurrection of the unrighteous (Revelation 20:12-13).

## C. The Destiny of the Righteous

Jesus Himself described heaven as paradise when speaking to the thief on the cross: *Assuredly, I say to you, today you will be with Me in Paradise* (Luke 23:43). He also assures us in this verse that upon our death, we go immediately into the presence of God.

As Paul tells us in 2 Corinthians 5:8, *We are confident, yes, well pleased rather to be absent from the body and to be present with the Lord.* And, where is the Lord? In heaven: *But he* [Stephen], *being full of the Holy Spirit, gazed into heaven and saw the glory of God, and Jesus standing at the right hand of God* (Acts 7:55). The original word for *heaven* means "high or lofty," or "that which is above," which designates where heaven is located.

In heaven there will be no more pain, suffering or tears, for God will make all things new:

*And God will wipe away every tear from their eyes; there shall be no more death, nor sorrow, nor crying. There shall be no more pain, for the former things have passed away* (Revelation 21:4).

The Book of Revelation has many descriptions of heaven: the throne room in Revelation 4:2-3, *and behold, a throne set in heaven, and One sat on the throne. And He who sat there was like a jasper and a sardius stone in appearance; and there was a rainbow around the throne, in appearance like an emerald*; Jesus at the throne in Revelation 5:2-7; and the angels' worship of God in Revelation 5:8-14.

Following the final judgment—the Great White Throne Judgment—there will be a new heaven and a new earth, as the current heaven and earth are destroyed by fire (Revelation 21:1 and 2 Peter 3:10-13). Also described is the New Jerusalem, the final dwelling place that Christ has prepared for us, in which we have personal, intimate fellowship with Him throughout eternity (Revelation 21). The main point is that heaven is the place where we will live in the immediate presence of God, eternally.

## D. The Destiny of the Wicked

The Bible tells us of two places where the wicked will go. The first is *Hades* or *hell*, the temporary place, and the second is *Gehenna* or the *Lake of Fire*, the final place of torment. Although the Bible does not give us a detailed description of Hades or hell, it does tell us some truths about it. Jesus describes *hell* as a "place in the center of the earth:"

> *"So it was that the beggar died, and was carried by the angels to Abraham's bosom. The rich man also died and was buried. And being in torments in Hades, he lifted up his eyes and saw Abraham afar off, and Lazarus in his bosom. Then he cried and said, 'Father Abraham, have mercy on me, and send Lazarus that he may dip the tip of his finger in water and cool my tongue; for I am tormented in this flame' "* (Luke 16:22-24).

First, Scripture tells us that hell is only a temporary place for the wicked who await the final judgment—a place of torment, *when I* [the Lord God] *cast it down to hell together with those who descend into the Pit* (Ezekiel 31:16).

Then, after the final judgment, hell will be cast into the Lake of Fire, Gehenna:

> *The sea gave up the dead who were in it, and Death and Hades delivered up the dead who were in them. And they were judged, each one according to his works. Then Death and Hades were cast into the lake of fire. This is the second death* (Revelation 20:13-14).

Although the Lake of Fire was prepared for the devil and his demons, those who have died and chosen to reject Christ as their Lord and Savior will be in Hades or hell when it is cast into the Lake of Fire. In Matthew 25:41, Jesus taught, *"Then He will also say to those on the left hand, 'Depart from Me, you cursed, into the everlasting fire prepared for the devil and his angels.' "*

The Bible tells us that those who go to the Lake of Fire will never die, but live in torment forever and ever, eternally separated from God. The Gospel of Mark says, *where their worm does not die, And the fire is not quenched* (Mark 9:44, 46, 48).

The Bible also teaches that there will be degrees of suffering in hell and the final judgment. Some unbelievers are going to be more accountable for what they have received and for the things they have done (Luke 12:47-48; Matthew 11:22-24).

While believers will be resurrected with glorified, incorruptible bodies, it is assumed that unbelievers will be raised with corruptible bodies that are subject to suffering, eternally:

> *The Lord Jesus is revealed from heaven with His mighty angels, in flaming fire taking vengeance on those who do not know God, and on those who do not obey the gospel of our Lord Jesus Christ. These shall be punished with everlasting destruction from the presence of the Lord and from the glory of His power* (2 Thessalonians 1:8-9).

Because the unrighteous do not receive glorified bodies, they will still possess all five senses and will suffer. Jesus describes the suffering of the unrighteous in Matthew 25:30: *"And cast the unprofitable servant into the outer darkness. There will be weeping and gnashing of teeth."*

## E.  The Order of the Last Things

Before we look at the events of the Last Things, I would like to give you a brief outline of the sequence of events, beginning with the church departing from the earth, the Rapture, and ending with God making all things new. This will help you to understand the order of the last things:

**The Rapture**

**The Tribulation**

**The Second Coming of Christ**

**The Millennium**

**The Judgment**

**All Things Made New**

## F.  The Rapture

For many, the idea of the Rapture is confusing because the word *Rapture* is not found in the English Bible. What we have is the phrase *caught up* (1 Thessalonians 4:17). In Greek, the word used is *harpazo*, meaning "caught up" or "to be snatched away by force." In Latin, it is *raptus*, which is the word found in one of the oldest Bibles in existence, the Latin Vulgate. This Latin word *raptus* is where we get our English word, Rapture.

The Rapture of the church will take place when Christ descends in the clouds, raising those who have died as believers first. Then, those alive and living a Christian life will be caught up with Christ in the clouds:

> *For the Lord Himself will descend from heaven with a shout,*
> *with the voice of an archangel, and with the trumpet of God.*
> *And the dead in Christ will rise first. Then we who are alive*
> *and remain shall be caught up together with them in the clouds*
> *to meet the Lord in the air. And thus we shall always be with*
> *the Lord* (1 Thessalonians 4:16-17).

In order for the believers, both dead and alive to join Christ, we must be changed from flesh and blood into incorruptible, immortal bodies, for that which is corrupt cannot enter the heavenly realm (1 Corinthians 15:50-54). In this transition, death no longer holds the victory over the believer for we have victory in Christ (1 Corinthians 15:55-57). So, when the believers are caught up with Christ, they will receive their glorified, incorruptible bodies, just as the dead in Christ received theirs:

> *Behold, I tell you a mystery: We shall not all sleep, but we*
> *shall all be changed; in a moment, in the twinkling of an eye,*
> *at the last trumpet. For the trumpet will sound, and the dead*
> *will be raised incorruptible, and we shall be changed. For this*
> *corruptible must put on incorruption, and this mortal must put*
> *on immortality* (1 Corinthians 15:51-53).

No one knows the day or the hour of the Rapture: *of that day*
*and hour no one knows, not even the angels of heaven, but My Father*
*only* (Matthew 24:36); however, the Scriptures clearly tell us that there will be signs and we must be prepared:

> *But you, brethren, are not in darkness, so that this Day*
> *should overtake you as a thief. You are all sons of light and*
> *sons of the day. We are not of the night nor of darkness.*
> *Therefore let us not sleep, as others do, but let us watch and*
> *be sober. For those who sleep, sleep at night, and those who get*
> *drunk are drunk at night. But let us who are of the day be*
> *sober, putting on the breastplate of faith and love, and as a*
> *helmet the hope of salvation. For God did not appoint us to*
> *wrath, but to obtain salvation through our Lord Jesus Christ*
> (1 Thessalonians 5:4-9).

We can see from the Scriptures above that while we do not know when Christ is coming to take us up with Him, He does expect us to be prepared. It is necessary for us to be living according to His Word, waiting with great anticipation for His coming, *For our citizenship is in heaven, from which we also eagerly wait for the Savior, the Lord Jesus Christ* (Philippians 3:20).

A great Bible commentary writer, Matthew Henry, gives an explanation of perhaps why Jesus did not reveal the day or the hour: "Christ will come when He pleases, to show His sovereignty, and will not let us know when, to teach us our duty."

Christ knows the heart of man and desires we would live our lives in such a way that He could come at any time, and we would be ready—anticipating His return—living in the hope that we will see the people we love who have died before us.

## G. The Tribulation

Following the Rapture—the removal of the church from the earth, along with the departure of the Holy Spirit (2 Thessalonians 2:7)—a period of seven years, filled with great despair and devastation, will follow, called *The Tribulation*. Jesus, Himself spoke of this time in Matthew 24:6-9:

> *"And you will hear of wars and rumors of wars. See that you are not troubled; for all these things must come to pass, but the end is not yet . . . there will be famines, pestilences, and earthquakes . . . All these are the beginning of sorrows. "Then they will deliver you up to tribulation and kill you, and you will be hated by all nations for My name's sake."*

### 1. The Unholy Trinity

It is during this period that the "unholy trinity" will rise to power, led by *Satan,* who will establish a one-world government ruled by the *Antichrist*, and a one-world religion under the *False Prophet*.

J. Oswald Sanders explains this counterfeit trinity in, *Satan Is No Myth:*

Satan counterfeits what God does. Satan wanted to be like God and still does. In the Tribulation, Satan will have his own trinity. In Revelation 13 - there is the devil, that great dragon, who is an unholy father (13:4); there is the beast, the antichrist, who is an unholy son (13:1); and the third person of his trinity is the false prophet, the one who does lying signs and wonderful miraculous works, he's an unholy spirit [Revelation 19:20]. These three working together will deceive and control the entire world.

## 2.   The Abomination of Desolation

The Antichrist will negotiate peace between Israel and the Arab nations, allowing the Temple to be rebuilt upon the Temple Mount next to the Dome of the Rock—the Muslim shrine:

> *Then he shall confirm a covenant with many for one week; But in the middle of the week He shall bring an end to sacrifice and offering. And on the wing of abominations shall be one who makes desolate, Even until the consummation, which is determined, Is poured out on the desolate* (Daniel 9:27).

In the verse above, Daniel speaks of a period of *one week*. This week is in reference to the "seven years of Tribulation." The Tribulation begins when the Antichrist makes a covenant with Israel and helps her rebuild the Temple. However, in the middle of the seven years, the Antichrist will break his covenant. He will set himself up as God in the temple and seek to force the Jews and the world to worship him (2 Thessalonians 2:4). This will be such an abomination to God that He will bring desolation on the earth. That is why the Bible calls it the *abomination of desolation*. Jesus explained: *"Therefore when you see the 'abomination of desolation,' spoken of by Daniel the prophet, standing in the holy place"* (whoever reads, let him understand) (Matthew 24:15).

The second half of the seven years is known as *The Great Tribulation*, as explained by Jesus:

> *"For then there will be great tribulation, such as has not been since the beginning of the world until this time, no, nor ever shall be. And unless those days were shortened, no flesh would be saved; but for the elect's sake those days will be shortened"* (Matthew 24:21-22).

During this period, God will be dealing with the Jewish Nation, and many of them will come to the saving knowledge of Jesus Christ, recognizing that they missed the First Coming of the Messiah.

While the Antichrist will bring great persecution against the Nation of Israel (Daniel 7:25), God will seal His remnant of 144,000 Jews from the twelve tribes (Revelation 7:1-8), and protect His people (Revelation 12:6).

At that time, many people from around the world will become Tribulation Saints. These are unbelievers who had been left behind during the Rapture and became believers when they accepted Christ as their Savior during the Tribulation (Revelation 7:9-17).

### 3. God's Judgments
The Tribulation, the last seven years of world history, will also be marked by the judgments of God, as He pours out His wrath upon the earth.

    a.  The Judgments of the Seven Seals:
        Revelation 6:1 - 8:1
    b.  The Judgments of the Seven Trumpets:
        Revelation 8:6 - 11:15
    c.  The Abomination of Desolation:
        Matthew 24:15
    d.  The Judgments of the Seven Bowls of Wrath:
        Revelation 15 - 16
    e.  The Judgment of the Harlot: Revelation 17 - 18

At the end of the Tribulation, the nations of the East will join the armies of the Antichrist and come against the remnant of Israel in the *Battle of Armageddon* (Revelation 16:12-16). However, they will be defeated, as Christ returns with His armies of saints to completely destroy the armies of the Antichrist; this is the Second Coming of Christ (Revelation 19:14-21):

> *And then the lawless one* [the Antichrist] *will be revealed, whom the Lord will consume with the breath of His mouth and destroy with the brightness of His coming* (2 Thessalonians 2:8).

## H. The Second Coming of Jesus Christ

*Behold, He is coming with clouds, and every eye will see Him, even they who pierced Him. And all the tribes of the earth will mourn because of Him* (Revelation 1:7).

The Second Coming of Jesus Christ is one of the most important doctrines of the New Testament, mentioned more than 300 times. With so much written about Christ's Second Coming, it is clear that the Lord wants Christians to be aware of what it means and what will take place.

With this in mind, let's look at what the Scriptures tell us about what it is, when it will happen and what will occur.

### 1.   What is the Second Coming?

The *Second Coming of Christ* is not something that is figurative; it is "the literal, physical return of Jesus to the earth." In His First Coming, Jesus humbly came to this earth to be born, live among us, die for our sins, resurrect and give new life, thus fulfilling Bible prophecy. However, the Bible tells us that at His Second Coming, Jesus will come to the earth again in great power and great glory:

*Now when Jesus had spoken these things, while they watched, He was taken up, and a cloud received Him out of their sight. And while they looked steadfastly toward heaven as He went up, behold, two men stood by them in white apparel, who also said, "Men of Galilee, why do you stand gazing up into heaven? This same Jesus, who was taken up from you into heaven, will so come in like manner as you saw Him go into heaven"* (Acts 1:9-11).

*For the Son of Man will come in the glory of His Father with His angels, and then He will reward each according to his work* (Matthew 16:27).

It is very important to keep in mind the difference between the Second Coming and the earlier event of the Rapture of the Church. The Rapture and Second Coming are similar in that they are both "comings" of Jesus, but they are two separate and distinct events. The Rapture is the coming of Jesus *for* His saints (1 Thessalonians 4:16-17); whereas the Second Coming is the coming of Jesus *with* His saints (1 Thessalonians 3:13; Jude 14).

The Rapture happens right before the Tribulation; the Second Coming happens at the end of the Tribulation. At the Rapture, believers will meet the Lord in the air, but at the Second Coming, Jesus will come all the way to the earth. The Rapture is imminent and could happen at any moment, but the Second Coming follows the Tribulation.

## 2. The Time of the Second Coming of Christ

When the Second Coming will happen depends on when the Tribulation begins. We do not know when the Rapture of the Church will happen (1 Thessalonians 5:1-6). It could happen on any day and at any moment (Matthew 24:36). But, the Second Coming of Christ follows definite, predicted signs, especially the events of the Tribulation: *So you also, when you see these things happening, know that the kingdom of God is near* (Luke 21:31). What are the signs and when will the Second Coming happen?

The seven year period of the Tribulation will begin when the Antichrist makes a covenant of peace with Israel and helps her rebuild the temple in Jerusalem (Daniel 9:27). Then in the middle of the Tribulation, the Antichrist will set himself up as god in the temple and force the world to worship him (2 Thessalonians 2:4).

This event will be such an abomination that God will desolate the earth in judgment. That is why it is known as the Abomination of Desolation (Matthew 24:15). So, three and a half years after the Tribulation begins, the Abomination of Desolation will occur.

Then the Book of Daniel ends with an amazingly precise prophecy about the events surrounding the Second Coming:

> *And he said, "Go your way, Daniel, for the words are closed up and sealed till the time of the end. Many shall be purified, made white, and refined, but the wicked shall do wickedly; and none of the wicked shall understand, but the wise shall understand. And from the time that the daily sacrifice is taken away, and the abomination of desolation is set up, there shall be one thousand two hundred and ninety days. Blessed is he who waits, and comes to the one thousand three hundred and thirty-five days"* (Daniel 12:9-12).

Two specific times are mentioned in this passage—1,290 days and 1,335 days. Will the Second Coming be 1,290 days after the Abomination of Desolation or 1,335 days? And how do these time markers relate to the mention of 1,260 days in Revelation 11:3 and 12:6?

In Bible days, a year was considered 360 days. So 3 ½ years would be 1,260 days. This is why Revelation 11:3 and 12:6, indicate that the Second Coming of Christ will be 1,260 days after the Abomination of Desolation.

Revelation 13:5 seems to confirm this, mentioning 42 months, which again is 3 ½ years. This 3 ½ year time marker is also alluded to in the interesting phrase, *time, times, and a half a time*, as it appears in Daniel 7:25. In this phrase, *time* refers to "a year." So *time* is one year, *times* is "two years," and *half a time* is "half of a year." *Time, times, and half a time*, then, is 3 ½ years. All this seems to show that the Second Coming of Christ will be 1,260 days, or 3 ½ years, after the Abomination of Desolation.

Why then is Daniel told about 1,290 days and 1,335 days in Daniel 12:11-12? It seems clear that the Second Coming of Christ will be 1,260 days after the Abomination of Desolation. Then 1,290 days after the Abomination of Desolation, Jesus will set up His government in Jerusalem.

Why the 30 day gap? It may be that the 30 days between the Second Coming and the setting up of Christ's kingdom are to clean up the land of Israel after the Battle of Armageddon and purify the defiled temple.

Then Christ will judge the nations from His throne in Jerusalem, determining those who will enter the Millennial Kingdom and those who will not (Matthew 25:31-46; Joel 3:2). It seems that this judgment will take another 45 days, ending 1,335 days after the Abomination of Desolation. This is why Daniel is told, *Blessed is he who waits, and comes to the one thousand three hundred and thirty-five days* (Daniel 12:12), for those are the ones who will go into the Millennium and experience the blessing of Christ reigning as King on the earth.

What an awesome moment it will be when Jesus returns to this earth. The Bible tells us that when His feet touch down on the Mount of Olives, it will split in two, and a river will run backward into the Dead Sea, healing the waters and making it alive (Ezekiel 47:8-9):

*And in that day it shall be That living waters shall flow from Jerusalem, Half of them toward the eastern sea And half of them toward the western sea; In both summer and winter it shall occur. And the LORD shall be King over all the earth. In that day it shall be; "The LORD is one," And His name one* (Zechariah 14:8-9).

### 3.   The Purpose for the Second Coming

At His First Coming, Jesus came to bring salvation; but at His *Second Coming*, He will come "to bring judgment." At the end of the Tribulation when the nations of the earth gather under the Antichrist against the nation of Israel and the Tribulation Saints, Christ will return to bring their rebellion to an end. This is what the Bible calls The Battle of Armageddon. The name *Armageddon* is an allusion to the Valley of Megiddo in the land of Israel, where this battle will take place:

*And I saw three unclean spirits like frogs coming out of the mouth of the dragon, out of the mouth of the beast, and out of the mouth of the false prophet. For they are spirits of demons, performing signs, which go out to the kings of the earth and of the whole world, to gather them to the battle of that great day of God Almighty . . . And they gathered them together to the place called in Hebrew, Armageddon* (Revelation 16:13-14,16).

*Now I saw heaven opened, and behold, a white horse. And He who sat on him was called Faithful and True, and in righteousness He judges and makes war . . . His name is called the Word of God . . . And the armies in heaven, clothed in fine linen, white and clean, followed Him on white horses. Now out of His mouth goes a sharp sword, that with it He should strike the nations . . . And I saw the beast, the kings of the earth, and their armies, gathered together to make war against Him who sat on the horse and against His army. Then the beast was captured, and with him the false prophet who worked signs in his presence, by which he deceived those who received the mark of the beast and those who worshiped his image. These two were cast alive into the lake of fire burning with brimstone. And the rest were killed with the sword which proceeded from the mouth of Him who sat on the horse. And all the birds were filled with their flesh* (Revelation 19:11-21).

Once Christ has squashed the rebellious armies of the Antichrist, He will bind Satan in chains and cast him into the bottomless pit, the Abyss, for 1,000 years:

*He laid hold of the dragon, that serpent of old, who is the Devil and Satan, and bound him for a thousand years; and he cast him into the bottomless pit, and shut him up, and set a seal on him, so that he should deceive the nations no more till the thousand years were finished. But after these things he must be released for a little while* (Revelation 20:2-3).

At this time, God will raise the Tribulation Saints who have survived the terrible judgments and persecution of the Antichrist and his leaders (Revelation 20:4). Christ will judge the nations of the world who have come against Him, and will establish His Kingdom in Jerusalem where He will reign for 1,000 years (Revelation 20:6).

# I. The Millennium

The word *millennium* simply means "one thousand years." It refers to the 1,000 year period after Christ's Second Coming, when Satan is bound in the Abyss, and Christ sets up His kingdom to rule and reign on this earth (Revelation 20:2). During this period, the saints who came *with* Christ at His Second Coming will be in their glorious bodies (1 Thessalonians 4:15-17; 1 Corinthians 15:50-53; Revelation 20:4,6).

It seems that those believers who survive the Great Tribulation will continue to be in their earthly bodies. Apparently, believers in the Millennium will not receive their glorified bodies until after the 1,000 years and the final judgment. Those in their earthly bodies will reproduce and repopulate the earth during the Millennium.

The main characteristic of the Millennial Kingdom will be peace. The nations will coexist in peace, animals will live together in peace, and it will be a time of joy, happiness and prosperity for all. It will be a time of perfect justice and righteousness, led by Jesus Christ:

> *And the LORD shall be King over all the earth. In that day it shall be; "The LORD is one," And His name one* (Zechariah 14:9).

> *But with righteousness He shall judge the poor, and decide with equity for the meek of the earth; He shall strike the earth with the rod of His mouth, and with the breath of His lips He shall slay the wicked. Righteousness shall be the belt of His loins, and faithfulness the belt of His waist. The wolf also shall dwell with the lamb, the leopard shall lie down with the young goat, the calf and the young lion and the fatling together; and a little child shall lead them. The cow and the bear shall graze; their young ones shall lie down together; and the lion shall eat straw like the ox. The nursing child shall play by the cobra's hole, and the weaned child shall put his hand in the viper's den. They shall not hurt nor destroy in all My holy mountain, for the earth shall be full of the knowledge of the LORD As the waters cover the sea. And in that day there shall be a Root of Jesse, Who shall stand as a banner to the people; for the Gentiles shall seek Him, and His resting place shall be glorious* (Isaiah 11:4-10).

God will fulfill His covenant with Israel at this time, as the nation experiences a time of great joy, prosperity, peace and longevity.

He will again establish the borders of the nation:

> *On the same day the LORD made a covenant with Abram, saying: "To your descendants I have given this land, from the river of Egypt to the great river, the River Euphrates; the Kenites, the Kenezzites, the Kadmonites, the Hittites, the Perizzites, the Rephaim, the Amorites, the Canaanites, the Girgashites, and the Jebusites"* (Genesis 15:18-21).

> God declared to His Son, *"Yet I have set My King on My holy hill of Zion. I will declare the decree: The LORD has said to Me, 'You are My Son, Today I have begotten You. Ask of Me, and I will give You The nations for Your inheritance, And the ends of the earth for Your possession. You shall break them with a rod of iron; You shall dash them to pieces like a potter's vessel' "* (Psalm 2:6-9).

> *Give the king Your judgments, O God, And Your righteousness to the king's Son. He will judge Your people with righteousness, And Your poor with justice. The mountains will bring peace to the people, and the little hills, by righteousness* (Psalm 72:1-3).

The first subjects of the rule of Christ on earth will be Jews and Gentiles who survive the Tribulation and enter the Kingdom in their earthly bodies. At the beginning of the Millennium, all the people on earth will be believers, for all unbelievers will have been judged at Christ's return. Those believers in their earthly bodies will repopulate the earth.

Those born in the Millennium will then have to decide their own spiritual relationship to Christ. Outwardly, all will have to be subject to Jesus as King; but inwardly, whether they accept Him as their Savior will be their decision. Eventually, there will be believers and unbelievers living in their earthly bodies during the Millennium.

## J.  The Judgment

At the end of the 1,000 year reign of Christ, Satan will be released from the bottomless pit and will go out to deceive the nations, drawing many into rebellion against Christ:

> *Now when the thousand years have expired, Satan will be released from his prison and will go out to deceive the nations which are in the four corners of the earth, Gog and Magog, to gather them together to battle, whose number is as the sand of the sea* (Revelation 20:7-8).

Remember, the believers who survive the Tribulation in their earthly bodies will repopulate the earth, and those born in the Millennium will have to decide their own spiritual relationship to Christ. It is unthinkable that these people will rebel and follow Satan after living in a perfect world with a perfect government, ruled by Jesus for 1,000 years, but they will. Because of their rebellious hearts, God's judgment will come down from heaven and destroy them: *And fire came down from God out of heaven and devoured them* (Revelation 20:9).

This rebellion is Satan's last stand. God will then cast him and his fallen angels into the Lake of Fire, with the Antichrist and the False Prophet, and he will no longer be allowed to stir up the nations in rebellion—instead, he will be tormented forever:

> *The devil, who deceived them, was cast into the lake of fire and brimstone where the beast and the false prophet are. And they will be tormented day and night forever and ever* (Revelation 20:10).

Once Satan is judged and condemned, God will turn to the judgment of all the unrighteous who ever lived—those who died who were not believers. This is called the *Great White Throne Judgment*. At this judgment, the unrighteous will be judged as to whether or not they have accepted God's gracious gift of eternal life. If their names are not found in the Book of Life, they will be cast into the Lake of Fire:

*Then I saw a great white throne and Him who sat on it, from whose face the earth and the heaven fled away. And there was found no place for them. And I saw the dead, small and great, standing before God, and books were opened. And another book was opened, which is the Book of Life. And the dead were judged according to their works, by the things which were written in the books. The sea gave up the dead who were in it, and Death and Hades delivered up the dead who were in them. And they were judged . . . And anyone not found written in the Book of Life was cast into the lake of fire* (Revelation 20:11-15).

The rebellious, those not found in the Book of Life, will experience eternity separated from God—in utter darkness (Matthew 22:13; 25:30).

## K. All Things Made New

After the Great White Throne Judgment, the first heaven and earth will pass away (Revelation 20:11). God will then make *all things new*—a new heaven, a new earth and a new Jerusalem.

Imagine how it will be when all things are made brand new. The things of this world, pain and suffering, will pass away for all those who are found written in the Book of Life—those who lived their lives steadfast in the Word of God. We have been called to be a holy people, set apart from the world, with a glorious promise—a life eternal with the Living God:

*Now I saw a new heaven and a new earth, for the first heaven and the first earth had passed away. Also there was no more sea. Then I, John, saw the holy city, New Jerusalem, coming down out of heaven from God, prepared as a bride adorned for her husband. And I heard a loud voice from heaven saying, "Behold, the tabernacle of God is with men, and He will dwell with them, and they shall be His people. God Himself will be with them and be their God"* (Revelation 21:1-3).

*"And God will wipe away every tear from their eyes;*

*there shall be no more death, nor sorrow, nor crying.*
*There shall be no more pain, for the former things have*
*passed away." Then He who sat on the throne said,*
*"Behold, I make all things new."*

Revelation 21:4-5

"Surely I AM coming quickly."
Amen. Even so, come, Lord Jesus!
The grace of our Lord Jesus Christ be with you all.
Amen.

Revelation 22:20-21

# BIBLIOGRAPHY

Blanchard, John. *More Gathered Gold*. Hertfordshire: Evangelical, 1986.

Duffield, Guy P., and Nathaniel M. Van Cleave. *Foundations of Pentecostal Theology*. Los Angeles: Foursquare Media, 2008.

Evans, William. *The Great Doctrines of the Bible*. Chicago: Moody, 1974.

Geisler, Norman L., and William E. Nix. *A General Introduction to the Bible*. Chicago: Moody, 1986.

Landau, Sidney I., ed. *The New International Webster's Family Dictionary of the English Language*. N.p.: Trident, 1999.

Pearlman, Myer. *Knowing the Doctrines of the Bible*. Springfield: Gospel, 2002.

Pentecost, J. Dwight. *Things to Come*. Grand Rapids: Zondervan, 1980.

Pentecost, J. Dwight. *Your Adversary the Devil*. Grand Rapids: Kregel, 1997.

Phillips, John, and Jerry Vines. *Exploring the Book of Daniel*. Neptune: Loizeaux Bros., 1990.

Rhodes, Ron. *Angels Among Us: Separating Fact from Fiction*. Eugene: Harvest, 2008.

Sanders, J. Oswald. *Satan Is No Myth*. Chicago: Moody, 1975.

Smith, Chuck. *Living Water: The Power of the Holy Spirit in Your Life*. Eugene: Harvest, 1996.

Smith, Chuck. *The Final Act: Setting the Stage of the End Times Drama*. Costa Mesa: Word for Today, 2007.

Smith, Chuck. *Through the Bible 2000*. MP3. Word for Today, 2007.

Strong, James, LL.D., S.T.D. *The New Strong's Exhaustive Concordance of the Bible*. Nashville: Nelson, 1990.

Torrey, R. A. *What the Bible Teaches*. New Kensington: Whitaker, 1996.

Vine, W. E. *The Expanded Vine's Expository Dictionary of New Testament Words*. Minneapolis: Bethany, 1984.

Williams, J. Rodman. *God, the World & Redemption*. Grand Rapids: Zondervan, 1988.

Williams, J. Rodman. *Salvation, the Holy Spirit, and Christian Living*. Grand Rapids: Zondervan, 1988

## PERSONAL LIBRARY SUGGESTIONS

*New King James Bible*

*Foundations of Pentecostal Theology*
by Guy Duffield and Nathaniel Van Cleave

*Strong's Exhaustive Concordance*

*Halley's Bible Handbook*

*Unger's Concise Bible Dictionary and Concordance*
by Merrill F. Unger

Basic Bible Commentary — i.e. Beacon's

*The Bible Knowledge Commentary*
by John Walvoord and Roy B. Zuck

Word Studies of the New Testament —
i.e. Vine's, Vincent's, Robertson's

*Nave's Topical Bible*

*Vine's Complete Expository Dictionary of Old Testament
and New Testament Words* by W.E. Vine

## OTHER READING MATERIALS

*The Great Doctrines of the Bible*
by William Evans

*What the Bible Teaches*
by R. A. Torrey

*Knowing the Doctrines of the Bible*
by Myer Pearlman

Chuck Smith
Through the Bible Studies C 2000 MP3
*The Word for Today Bible*
*Calvary Chapel Distinctives*
*Living Water*
*Calvinism, Armenianism, and the Word of God*
*Why Grace Changes Everything*
*The Final Act*

# Somebody Loves You Media Group

## BOOKS

### Raul Ries

*From Fury to Freedom*
*Raising a Godly Family in an Ungodly World*
*Hear What the Spirit Is Saying*
*Seven Steps to a Successful Marriage*
*God Answers Prayer*
*Five Deadly Vices*
*Understanding God's Compassion*
*Wake Up! Time Is Short*
*Follow Me*
*Practical Living from God's Word*
*Somebody Loves You Growth Book*

*Things of the Spiritual Realm:* Angels,
Physical Attacks, Satan and Warfare

*Living Above Your Circumstances* –
A Study in the Book of Daniel

### Sharon Ries

*My Husband, My Maker*
*The Well-Trodden Path*

### Various Authors

*Patriarcas en la Carcel*
by Ruth Smith
*The Philosophy of Ministry of Calvary Chapel*
by Chuck Smith

## FILMS IN DVD*

### Raul Ries

*Fury to Freedom*

*Taking the Hill:* A Warrior's Journey Home

*A Quiet Hope:* A Film for Vietnam Veterans

*A Venture in Faith:* The History and Philosophy
of the Calvary Chapel Movement

*All DVD's are in English and Spanish

Somebody Loves You Media Group
22324 Golden Springs Drive
Diamond Bar, CA 91765-2449

(800) 634-9165
slymediagroup@somebodylovesyou.com
www.somebodylovesyou.com